THE FAITH IN PURITY

TIMOTHY POMP

Copyright 2022 by Timothy Pomp

All rights reserved. No part of this publication may be reproduced, stored or transmitted in any form or by any means, electronic, mechanical, photocopying, recording, scanning, or otherwise without written permission from the publisher. It is illegal to copy this book, post it to a website, or distribute it by any other means without permission.

First published by Swift Word Publishing 02.22.2022

All Scripture taken from the New King James Version® unless otherwise noted. Copyright © 1982 by Thomas Nelson. Used by permission. All rights reserved.

Cover Design by Gina Nielsen, Amity Graphics

ISBN: 978-1-945121-21-0 (paperback)

CONTENTS

Forward	v
Preface	ix
Introduction	xiv
The 2:22 Secret	1
Enemies of Purity	5
A living Sacrifice	9
Christ has redeemed us from the curse	14
His Desires, My Desires?	19
Opening the Gate of Grace	23
The Holy Spirit vs Pretense	27
Uncovering All Pride	31
Deep Secrets, or Secret Sins	35
Grace, Grace, Grace - He's Coming Soon	39
The Gift Of Resolve (Part 1)	43
The Gift Of Resolve (Part 2)	48
The Gift Of Resolve (Part 3)	52
Go To The Ant You Sluggard	56
Adultery	61
The Baptism of the Holy Spirit (Part 1)	65
The Baptism of the Holy Spirit (Part 2)	69
Proven Character	74
Put On Him, Put Off ME	80

Pursue A Pure Heart	85
The Sufferings Of Christ	92
What If	96
The Faith In Purity	100
He That Overcometh	104
The Number 22	109
Prophesying Over My Potential	116
Two Ways: Wide and Easy or Narrow and Difficult	120
Exposing Shame	126
Pulling Down Strongholds	130
Goliath Must Fall, (Part 1)	134
Goliath Must Fall (Part 2)	139
The Sin Of The Religious Spirit (Part 1)	143
The Sin Of The Religious Spirit (Part 2)	148
Partners With Conscience	154

Forward

   Tim Pomp has a history of friendship with the Holy Spirit and it shows. If I didn't know the working title of the book I would have thought it was called, "Stubborn Hope - Finding Purity in an Impure Culture" I've known Tim for many years and his dynamic preaching and infectious joy would certainly set him up as a candidate for positions of influence in any city God called him to. But instead, Tim has humbly answered the call to places on the map most of us have never heard of and will likely never visit. To the people of these places, far from airports and throngs of tourists, Tim has given his life to serve. I would say this book represents that life well. When a minister of the Gospel cultivates a secret place with the Lord, where time and attention are given to prayer and study of the Word, it produces insights, wisdom, and revelation. But, in my life, only a small percentage of the things revealed in that secret place ever get shared publicly. I imagine the same is true for Tim as well. When you're in covenant with someone, the secrets of their heart become your most cherished treasure. We have been brought into a new covenant in Christ, and the secrets of his heart are the inheritance of the disciple who has seen into those eyes of love. Just one look and you're never the same. It's in that place that you learn to hear his voice, and the sound exchanged in those conversations is the wisdom that shapes a life.

Tim Pomp has been shaped by the voice of the Lord. These are more than principles. They're your opportunity to listen in on conversations between a son and his Heavenly Father. Most of those conversations are deeply personal, and produce a life of discipline rooted in love and the fear of the Lord. That intimacy is the reward of a covenant relationship with God. In these pages, you'll get to peer behind the veil of an authentic modern day disciple of Jesus Christ, and what you see will challenge and encourage you. As I read this book, I couldn't help but feel as though I was overhearing nuggets of truth and wisdom from decades of Tim's secret place conversations with God. This book is a beautiful blend of righteousness, peace, and joy in the Holy Spirit. It's a Kingdom living discipleship manual that will inspire you to pursue your own secret place relationship with God.

Bill Vanderbush
Author/Speaker

WHAT OTHERS ARE SAYING

This book has something for everybody - from the newest to the most mature believer. Tim has achieved the goal of not only telling us what the Scripture asks of us but shows us how to achieve the goal. Through personal example and Holy Spirit inspired insights, you will be challenged and encouraged to personally discover and experience The Faith in Purity.

Ian Peters
Apostolic Overseer, Global Apostolic Alliance

I am convinced that there is no better time than now for this book by my friend Tim. You will find that he brings out the significance of the number 22 throughout scripture, of course published in the year of 2022. But it is so much more than just the timing of our calendar. It "is for such a time as this", for drawing closer to the purposes of the Kingdom of God. This is a study that leads the reader to look in depth at the significant 2:22 verses throughout the Bible, with a focus on the dynamic value of living pure in heart. The challenges to this life-giving, power-filled walk, are presented in context with embracing hope and a longing for the inner work of the Holy Spirit. I pray that you will experience Isaiah 22:22 as you read this treatise... an open door that no one can shut!

Mike Smith
Senior Pastor, Redeeming Love Church, St. Paul, MN

Preface

"Where are those delightful dark chocolates, dear"? And with a little grin on her face, "they are hidden in a secret spot my beloved"! Hidden things usually symbolize either treasure or nightmares. Secrets sometimes have a source of a person or Father that is teaching a lesson. Sometimes hidden hurts can grow into negative strongholds. The Lord's secrets are something special, beyond the norm, exceeding surface communication. Take Father God for example: Proverbs 25:2a-It is the glory of God to conceal a matter, but the glory of kings to search it out.

So I'd like to journey with you into the secret treasures of FAITH. The disciples cried to Jesus; increase our faith. He would eventually say through Paul that it is impossible to please me without faith, you can remove mountains with this substance. Faith with grace will be the ticket to an eternal home and countless blessings, and true faith will express itself through love. But In a picture, He sat a child on His lap and said; become like this. A pure innocent child without the barriers of status, skill and education. Simply trust Me and you will uncover the greatest secret known to man, the Kingdom of God!! We must desire and vehemently pursue strong faith.

"The kingdom of God suffers violence, and the violent take it by force" I begin, and at the end of this journey we will see that faith is an action verb. In a culture of "in your face" government, social media, and blatant lies trying to rule the world, faith must come to act in each moment of our lives. I recently had to take my calendar off my iPhone because I was hacked directly with porn offers in my calendar that I did not solicit. I don't even understand what happened, but it is a powerful example of what we deal with today. My beloved and I talked about it and are finding answers.

So let me define PURITY in context to this violent overtake. I want to take you on a journey of boldness and shouting walls of defilement and shame until Jericho is destroyed. Jericho and its walls, and mandates, PERFECTLY define the blatant spirit of this world! God's trumpet blast and man's shout must come against everyday walls of fear, shame, and sin.

Let's briefly examine the account of Jericho. When the Israelites took Jericho, NO SPOILS WERE TO BE KEPT. EVERYTHING was to be destroyed. A SECRET chunk of gold hidden by Achan put a curse on the entire tribe, and his family was executed. The first city (said to be the oldest city in history) was entirely sacrificed to the Father. Jericho was never to be rebuilt.

The one man's impurity after the fall of Jericho destroyed his family and dire consequences to Israel. This is a prime illustration of impurity in our personal life. When Christ becomes Lord, He is to remain the only God, no others before HIM.

This book is the first part of three books that will be coming. This first of the trilogy will be unveiling the Secret code 2:22. I'd like you to journey with me to consider this thought, strong faith cannot exist without purity. A song from decades ago said, purity and victory, you cannot separate them. Faith works by love! Purity is our language to Father that we love him. I desire to activate your creativity, and discover the gold mine of God's word to cleanse our lives.

The second book will focus on honoring Father God by putting Him first in every part of our lives. We must understand every vice that would come against Him being first. When you put Him first, you open the doors of destiny created for you. This study will comprehensively look into the first chapters of the epistles.

The third book will focus on the Lion of the tribe of Judah. We will cover the concept of the violent take it by force. Jesus Christ violently conquered death, hell, and the grave as He gave Himself as a sacrifice. Christianity is not for wimps! My friends, you will not prevail in this life if you are not IN JESUS CHRIST, and if you shrink back from His Kingdom, He takes no pleasure in you. Heb 10:38

Come along on this journey as this book is about absolute change. This is about FAITH, without which I cannot please God. Understanding this FAITH IN PURITY will change your life.

I want to dedicate this manuscript to my incredible son and daughter, who are currently 33 and 29 years old. I love you, Timmer and Johanna! Indeed, most Gen-Exers and Millennial's remain stuck behind Jericho's walls or still stuck in the wilderness. Through this book, I'm asking you to forge over that Jordan river into the promised land. Joshua and Caleb stood looking at the good land promised them. They had a choice of what to focus on. What do you see? What can you imagine? A land full of brutal giants, or a glorious land, grapes the size of golf balls.

If you can focus on the 'promised land,' you'll still need the tools to win the battles. I want to give you WORD tools! But the main focus of this book will not be to lecture about sexual purity or the impurity involved in addiction, worldliness, and corruption. Instead, throughout these pages, we'll discover the tools God has given you through His Word and how to connect with the Holy

Spirit. To discover hidden vices that only come from digging into Father, Jesus, and Spirit.

It may be tempting to give up on this challenging teaching, but a heart change can occur if the principles of this book are ingested. My goal is to teach you how to unveil the secrets of your heart and find victory on the path to freedom.

The book of Colossians shouts to mortify, or kill, violently, put to death the flesh! My cry to Jesus is to "Be Holy As He Is Holy. I think hypocrisy is the greatest act of impurity and hindrance to faith. This spirit undermines the real God to make itself one! It's time for the Bride to make Herself ready. It's time for purity. He's coming for a pure bride.

This book is laid out to spend maybe 5-7 minutes on each chapter (depending on how much you dig) with a thought, story, principle bathed in scripture about FAITH IN PURITY. I will quickly unveil the SECRET 2:22, and the first chapters will focus on twenty of the verses that have the reference 2:22. The last dozen chapters will bring revelation through topics such as motives, resolve, forgiveness, defraud, pretense, and conscience.

Introduction

I begin this study in the word of God, reflecting on three remarkable stories of faith in the bible. The paradigm for my life is hope and probably will always be. The secret of HOPE that has the DNA to become FAITH. As we get started, please, please strengthen your hope and expectation. It is the catalyst to your life of faith. If this is not a typical introduction, I want you to know that the Word of God is my ONLY PRIORITY.

These are characters who did not have biblical education and spiritual insight. They were regular people like us. Yet, they had HEARD A WORD OF HOPE and would climb a mountain of opposition and push past multitudes, to stand before Jesus. The Easter egg hunt is on, and the one who searches the most diligently will find the secrets. I ask the Holy Spirit to bring you Pure Hope and true miracles as you dive into THE FAITH IN PURITY.

Let your own faith be stirred as we read about these everyday people.

Our first story begins with a lady that heard the news about the messiah being nearby. She may have journeyed for days to find this Messiah, knowing He could deliver her daughter that was full of demons. In today's world, we have a plethora of drugs that would numb the pain. But she fought day and night in a battle of rage, abuse, and trauma. Then one day, the word came of blind eyes opened, the lame walking, and deaf hearing. It spread like wildfire. Tens of thousands heard the same reports, and one only had the audacity to follow hope and walk and walk until she fell at His table.

We can see her pure hope is the only thing that fought through her opposition. Jesus seems to ignore her, and then calls her a dog, "why should I give you my crumbs?" She responded, "no worries, call me anything you want, but my stubborn hope tells me that your crumbs will heal my daughter." I will take the crumbs of healing. Jesus responded, "You have great faith; let it be done to you AS YOU DESIRE." I love this so much, her daughter wasn't just healed; the trauma was over! Today I see the vision of your miracle exploding as you fall at His table.

The following story is about a woman who was a Jew and again heard reports and rumors that stirred hope—twelve years being unclean according to Jewish law. She was not just sick; she was a total outcast and unclean for twelve years with an issue of blood. Once again, her bullheaded fury to illegally walk (because she was unclean) through the streets to find a piece of fabric on the

Messiah is astounding. Yet, she had something that thousands who were present did not have, pure hope. Remember, it was not faith yet. When it is tangible, it is faith.

Jesus seemed willing to go anywhere and serve folks who were sick. He was marching with the massive crowd to heal Jairus' daughter. Jesus never declared Jairus to have great faith. So, this woman said, "if I can just touch His Garment." Her HOPE simply had a plan, THROUGH A VISION to touch Him, and she would be healed. She ruthlessly pushed and crawled, touched that garment, and the bible says, "she felt her body being healed." Some Peter dramas in between, but finally the glance from Messiah, and affirmation "your Faith has made you whole." Again, the difference between her and a multitude was a dose of pure hope attached to desire. Today, may you not faint in your pursuit of His garment. Remember what Jesus said, whatever you desire in my name, it will be done, John 15:7.

Then there was the Centurion. The subject of authority is significant in this story. Faith comes by hearing the Word of God. Again in these stories, pure hope pursued Jesus, Jesus did not pursue. Thousands had hope, but the critical mass moment comes when one pushes through every obstacle and receives from Jesus. This covers healing, salvation, forgiveness, direction, finances, etc.

Critical mass is the tiny fissile material needed to sustain a nuclear reaction. When he approached Jesus, he did not need the recognition of Jesus coming with him, he needed the fissile word of Hope from Jesus. After humility, and request, the affirmation came from Jesus; "as you have believed, so it will be done. I have not seen this faith even in Israel". The nuclear miracle needed no time or space, it was done! May we discover that this faith comes through pure motives, pure hope will explode into faith.

My utmost prayer is that hunger for God's Word and a desire for Lordship to Jesus would keep us from the Pharisee spirit and impurities of any kind. Please join me in this journey in continuing hope and its pure journey to faith. Hope also explodes into love (Roman 5:5), "Now hope does not disappoint, because the love of God has been poured out in our hearts by the Holy Spirit who was given to us." The heartbeat of this book is to teach us to transform pure hope into pure faith and love. (The following is from my previous book (The Greatest Measure, The Incredible, Eternal Quality of Hope) in the chapter "defining hope".

Hope is the hearing of faith; hope is the seeing in doing. Hope is in, Hope is on, Hope is through, and Hope defines the process. Hope is the expectation, the drive, the pistons, and the dividing light from the darkness. Hope is the clapping, the dancing, the shouting, the kneeling, and the expression of your heart. Faith and Love will transform from those expressions that have occurred. God's Hope is not wishful thinking.

Hope is insight, persistence, and stubborn bullheadedness. Hope is a confident expectation based on solid certainty.

Hope is the happy anticipation of good. Hope is the make-up of faith, the preface to faith, and the extension of faith.

Hope is confident in grace's future accomplishment. Hope is the verb side of grace; grace acts out, breathes, and gives hope.

Hope is crying, praying, waiting, and travailing until your Isaac has been birthed from a miracle called grace.

Hope is that God can give a door of hope even in utter tragedy and stupidity. Hope is an expectation, yearning for, and in anticipation, eagerly waiting. Hope is something for which one waits to bind together by twisting.

Hope is the speaking, confessing, singing expected from your lips as you stand against the enemy, hope is facing cancer, sickness, disease, or depression, but grabbing and clinching the healing from Jesus even before you have the manifestation. Hope is not giving in through symptoms, circumstances, doubts, fears. When even torment from the enemy has weakened you, hope does not give in. Hope is the joy of the Lord. Hope is the peace that passes understanding which is your strength. Faith is the moment of healing and restoration, yes that substance in your possession of what you saw through hope, and believed for, AMEN

Hope is smelling the bread of life.

Hope is thirsting for the water of life.

Hope is hungering for the meat and maturity of life.

Hope is touching the hem of Jesus' garment; faith receives virtue from Him. Love is looking into Jesus' eyes after He has healed you and you melt in your place.

Hope is what we are saved in (Romans 8:24).

Hope is our Anchor, but we are secured to the Faithful and Loving Rock, Jesus Christ.

Hope is embracing the Father God and knowing His embrace. Hope is defining the curse and receiving Christ's redemption. Hope is reflecting on Him with thanksgiving.

Hope is sacrificed to Him through praise. Hope is the planting of God's seed.

Hope is the dying of the seed.

Hope is the resurrecting of the seed.

Hope is weathering the storms after you've popped through the soil.

Hope is waiting for your purpose [fruit] to manifest and endure its tests.

Hope is waiting for ripened fruit until it has manifested. Faith and love are that fruit in you that identifies a true disciple.

Hope is the tasting of the Holy Spirit; love is embracing Him. Hope is expecting the promise, water, submersion, and the fire of the Holy Spirit.

Hope is the desire to be sealed by the Holy Spirit. Hope is developing Spirit fruit, the proof of that seal. Hope is patient, kind, and the process of never being jealous, boastful, or proud.

Hope is bearing all things, endures all things. Hope is the long process of developing your faith and love.

Hope is the assurance that in the father's timing Love and faith will come. So without faith, it is impossible to please God, this book is about moving on to faith with a pure motive.

XXII

THE CLOCK STRIKES 2:22
The 2:22 Secret

SCRIPTURAL FOUNDATION
1 JOHN 5:14B SAYS, ASK ANYTHING ACCORDING TO HIS WILL, AND HE HEARS US.

THE SECRET: YOU ARE SPECIAL

What is HOPE? It is the preface of faith, the make-up of faith, and the start of a new faith. Do not ever stop expecting and waiting, on the Lord, it will become THE FAITH IN PURITY. So, let's begin with the story of the 2:22 secret. No kidding, I can't prove this, but it could have been 22 years ago. I would have been 38 or 39. I know I was asking the Holy Spirit to open the doors of freedom. I would describe myself as a Spirit-Filled believer and weary from busy schedules, and at times fighting fear, shame, and youthful lusts.

A snapshot of me at 38 would be: growing in a

marriage with an incredible woman, using my gifts for his glory, growing in ministry, winning souls, and leading people into worship. But I struggled with lukewarmness, posing, and hiding fear and shame. At times I realize how powerful the fear of man affects the destiny of one's life. I so clearly want you to see that each person has different battles and vices, our aim is to mine out bad root systems that exist in us all, and DESTROY!

I remember that I was memorizing God's Word, and I genuinely do love His Word. I love to worship and be in His presence. And one blessed night, I had been asking the Lord to continue to give me tools to keep my Heart Pure. So, I went to bed one night; AND THEN IT HAPPENED. I woke up as if slapped across the face or, like a siren went off. I sat up in bed, and my eyes went straight to the digital clock. I was awakened out of a deep sleep, the clock said 2:22. SO WHAT?

It's easy for some to believe this could all have been a coincidence. However, today, I firmly believe that as I unfold this revelation, only the Holy Spirit could have orchestrated waking me at 2:22 to emphasize what I heard the Holy Spirit say next. It came, not an earthquake, not a strong wind, not a fire, but a still small voice breathed something as clear as a bell. "Tomorrow, when you get up, go through the entire bible, and check all the references of 2:22".

I was like, "OK", and I fell back to sleep. Yes, I woke up nice and early, and yes, I opened the Word, and yes, I knew because of my knowledge of 2 Tim. 2:22, that He was referring to my passion and lust. I also know a lot of scripture, by heart, and specific references. I remember thinking there may be 4-5 verses that have the reference of 2:22 that have a connotation to workings of the flesh. Well, I searched that day, and to my utter amazement, I discovered over 20 references in the bible that would address the subject of the workings of the flesh, 20 of which I will be expounding for you. Each one has the reference, chapter, and verse 2:22.

Interesting, the Lord would put this in a book published in 2022! There are also some powerful chapters in the Bible with 22 and 22:22. Like Psalms 22, the perfect prophetic cross chapter, and Isaiah 22:22, which says "the key of the house of David will I lay upon his shoulder; so he shall open, and none shall shut, and he shall shut, and none shall open." Thank you Jesus for opening this door!

So if there are 66 books in the Bible, is it possible that a third of them with a reference to 2:22, have been unveiled just for me. He cared just to share this secret with me, and I'd like to bless you. Maybe no one on the earth has ever seen this secret. And I believe your life will be changed. I believe you will receive keys that will unlock doors toward INCREDIBLY STRONG FAITH IN YOUR LIFE. One of our passages will be James 2:22, "Do you see that faith was working together with his works, and faith was made perfect by works?" May we discover those keys, and may we have the wisdom to open the doors.

Holy Spirit, you are here to change my life, give me tools to win over my flesh, and grow my faith. Let us all start with asking this question, "do I need more tools to produce strong faith?"

I ask you Lord to send your fire and begin a purging work in me which will result in strong faith. In Christ name, AMEN

CHAPTER ONE
Enemies of Purity

Scripture Foundation

1 Timothy 1:7a God has not given us fear.

THE SECRET: CLOTHED WITH GLORY

Genesis 2:22 (Winning over shame and fear) Then the rib which the LORD God had taken from man He made into a woman, and He brought her to the man.

This is where it all began. Can you only imagine the first moment Adam looked at Eve. Let's look at this moment in context to faith and purity, and God's holy DNA from the start. Woman was made out of the rib of man to be alongside. In our study, I will remind you that heaven is our ultimate destiny, in His presence. Heaven's clothes, as in the garden, will be "glory." Yes, they were naked, clothed with glory, and shame and fear DID NOT EXIST. Our ultimate goal of FREEDOM is to gaze without shame and fear, but with eyes through the Glory of the resurrection. The origin of man's purity was in this moment. The origin of authority and faith came as Father established the Family, man, and woman.

Everything there was Holy, and wrong passion was not possible until sin (separation) came on the scene. Oh, what a great verse to begin this teaching. We must be clothed with Glory again; shame and fear cannot exist in His LIGHT. We are born again of an incorruptible seed. Purity will cause that seed to grow out of your spirit and dominate your life. Men, He has caused you to honor one woman, and enjoy, and multiply unless He has called you to be celibate. If you are celibate, you are literally married to Jesus, and the way I see it, have no desire for the sexual union with another. The other choice, purity will be our goal, the holy bubble (glory) to surround you and that "one other."

So, let's again define purity in context to this moment. Father was saying, I have made man for fellowship, and first of all union with ONE spouse. Physical union is 2-fold, for your pleasure, and to populate the earth. Our first paramount key to Faith in purity is spirit to spirit Communication. Obviously with your Creator, but also your spouse.

When that is broken, the union will not survive. What is being born again? To become married to Christ spirit-to Spirit, and you MUST LEARN HOW TO TALK WITH OTHERS SPIRIT-TO-SPIRIT. Sex before marriage and looking wrong is directly breaking God's purpose of spirit-to-spirit union. (Matt. 5:28)

When impurity came through sin, then 1. His glory was almost immediately INVADED with fear and shame. 2. Understanding was lifted from the eyes. 3. Humility was changed to selfish pride, (excuses) 4. Truth was diluted and compromised, 5. Hypocrisy and the blame game became the cover, a fig leaf tried to replace holiness. James. 1:15-(my paraphrase) Eyes that desired the tree of knowledge of good and evil turned to SIN, and eventually DEATH. Yes, without hesitation, Adam also took and ate, and "they're eyes became open", and nakedness, fear and shame began its powerful onslaught.

So, as we dive into 2:22. There are a few enemies that we will attack with great fervency! Shame, which I define as the great thief of spirit-to-spirit relationships. A perfect picture of its ploy is "A MASK." The inability to look face-to-face and let Father's glory shine with Him and with others. In garden of Eden's lingo, it's a fig leaf, in today's lingo, it is a mask. Fear will be the other ancient enemy, and our goal will be to replace it with the FEAR

OF THE LORD. Next, we will expose, and define defraud. This word is very important to me. After 40 years of watching fear and shame, I have defined defraud as leading someone or yourself to a place where you cannot righteously fulfill your desires. Of course, the base word of defrauding is fraud. The mask and fraud concept was relevant even before Covid-19. Finally, we will expose another word that defines many sins in the body of Christ. It is the word pretense. Again, my definition: the successful attempt of a Christian to cover-up, hide, and elude the moral, godly intention of the Holy Spirit in you. Notice how the mask analogy also fits well with this. Understand that these enemies were born to destroy spirit-to-Spirit with Father, Son, Holy Spirit, and each other. Through the Faith in Purity, I aim to attack sins of anger, worry, religious pride, and prayerlessness, all fruits of fear and shame.

Holy Spirit, I ask you in Jesus' name to restore our original DNA. Your command to us; be perfect as I am perfect. (Matt. 5:48) Be Holy for I am Holy- (1Pet. 1:16) You made me righteous 2 Corinthians 5:21. In Jesus' name, restore the glory that surrounded Adam and Eve before the fall. Allow my status as the bride of Christ to stay pure, as You are coming for a pure bride. Open the eyes of my understanding, may fear and shame have no place in my life. In Christ Name, AMEN

CHAPTER TWO
A LIVING SACRIFICE

SCRIPTURE FOUNDATION

COLOSSIANS 3:5A THEREFORE PUT TO DEATH YOUR MEMBERS ON THE EARTH.

NUMBERS 2:22 (WINNING THE RIGHT BATTLE) THEN COMES THE TRIBE OF BENJAMIN, AND THE LEADER OF THE CHILDREN OF BENJAMIN SHALL BE ABIDAN THE SON OF GIDEONI."

SECRET: DEATH BRINGS LIFE

Remember the phrase, live by the sword or die by the sword. Military victory and violence go together. Well, Benjamin drew the military card of his eleven brothers. Jacob's twelve sons describe the Twelve Tribes of Israel and the first Israelite nation. Before he died, Jacob gave each son a prophetic blessing, describing the fate of their tribe. Of Benjamin, Jacob said:

"Benjamin is a ravenous wolf, devouring the prey in the morning and dividing the spoil at night." Alright then, thank you very much, dad, that's an exciting blessing! O dear son, you are a ravenous wolf! But you must understand how powerful this word is, especially as we begin this study.

Nehemiah 3:1a–the high priest arose with his brethren, the priests, and built the Sheep (Benjamin) Gate.

I would like to visit a mystery verse which I believe is important here. Matthew 11:12 says, the kingdom of heaven suffers violence, and the violent take it by force. In Book three, I will be addressing this subject in detail. Violence and sacrifice are secret codes to uncover your prophetic (like John the Baptist) paths to His kingdom.

What are the moments that purity is in jeopardy? High moments of victory, and times of achievement and pride, and moments of loneliness, and tragedies, when you feel you deserve a break. At times Satan stands in front of you with a temptation, and with full armor on, you swing your sword, and Satan flees. But in these times, you have your guard down. Proverbs 8:13 says, To fear the Lord is to (violently) hate evil (my emphasis). Stand up, fight for your purity, BE ANGRY AND SIN NOT!

Benjamin (and his people) would be fierce

warriors. However, the prophecy also made apparent the tribe's existence would be one of perpetual violence, day, and night. After Adam's sin, the Lord performed a first, violent, sacrifice of an animal, to "cover" the sins of the people. This is of course symbolic of the hope of a one-day perfect sacrifice of God's Son.

Benjamin and his purpose for faith in purity begins at the Benjamin Gate, a place of death. The battle is not against flesh and blood, but principalities and powers. Learning to die is truly the first and most important part of the Faith in Purity. The division of the spoil is significant in this book as we divide light and dark and embrace the light. It was called the sheep gate because this was the gate which the sheep and lambs were brought through to be sacrificed.

As the historic Jerusalem was being built, ten gates were set around the magnificent city of Peace. Though Benjamin was the last to be born of the twelve tribes, his gate, the sheep gate, marks the first as you move clockwise. Death to self must be first! This Gate speaks of the very first experience as we come into our Christian life. It speaks of the cross and the sacrifice that was made for our sins. The last Gate is the inspection Gate and represents the Quality test of our sacrifice as we march around the WALLS OF PEACE. Pure or impure, Holy, or unholy, weak faith or STRONG FAITH, pride, or humility! YOU CHOOSE BETWEEN EACH TWO!

Colossians 3:5 says, Put to death your members which are on the earth: fornication, uncleanness, passion, evil desire, and covetousness, which is idolatry. Because of these things, the wrath of God is coming upon the sons of disobedience.

Can it be any clearer; violently PUT TO DEATH? Remember Jesus said, "to look upon a woman to lust after her is fornication." Now carefully watch the bible's instructions. Colossians 3:8b-10 PUT OFF all these: anger, wrath, malice, blasphemy, filthy language out of your mouth. Do not lie to one another since you have put off the old man with his deeds and have put on the new man who is renewed in knowledge according to the image of Him who created him.

We must kill things, and some things will hang on and visit us until our last breath. Without the death of some things, you will not enter heaven, Revelation 21:8. Then other things will, according to Romans 12:1,2, be sacrificed. Since you will have anger and lies tempting you for the rest of your life, you must continually put them off. We must maintain and renew our mind, and the result, knowing His good, acceptable, and perfect will.

Holy Spirit, I give you my body a living sacrifice according to Romans 12:1, and I put to death today all the deeds of my flesh. Unveil the secret of me dying to self. However, I see that I am in a battle not with flesh and blood but with principalities and powers. I love you Lord, thank you for the strength and tools to win. I put on the breastplate of righteousness, the belt of truth, the shield of faith, the helmet of salvation, the sword of the Spirit, and I will pray all the time. In Christ name, AMEN

CHAPTER THREE
Christ has redeemed us from the curse

Scripture Foundation

Galatians 3:13-Christ has redeemed us from the curse of the law

Judges 2:22 - (Winning over generational curses) so that through them I may test Israel, whether they will keep the ways of the LORD, to walk in them as their fathers kept them."

SECRET: OBEDIENCE UNLOCKS ALL REDEEMING DOORS

According to Deuteronomy 5:9, Sin is passed to the 3rd & 4th generations. The bible says explicitly, "it visits." Isn't that interesting? You may be plugging along enjoying life, and suddenly, anger, lying, and a desire for a cigarette show up on your front door saying, "howdy, partner." How often have you said, "where did that (thought, word, action, desire) come from?" Your ability to keep the Ways of the Lord affects your children, great and great-great-grandchildren. I recommend that you have the blood of Christ painted on your door with a simple message, SIN NOT WELCOME HERE!

Is. 53:5 says He was wounded for our transgressions, He was bruised for our iniquities. Iniquity is defined, a passed down, multiplied sin. My thought: Jesus' nails and pierced side, He was wounded for our transgressions. His blood and water that flowed has historical power. It washed and cleansed fornication, idolatry, murder, transgressions. (Transgressions defined: missing the mark and being separated by acts of sin.) He was bruised for our iniquities. Iniquities would describe the beard pulling, beating, and bruising and those sins from Grandpa and Grandma. I believe it would include trauma, defilement, and sins of addiction, sins that are passed on. This sin is also passed on by you not applying the blood. Study David, Solomon, and Absalom, and the picture of iniquities becomes very clear. The issue is breaking the power of strongholds from your genes in Jesus' NAME. Also, we are called to embrace Judges 2:22a and keep firm the "ways of the Lord in our heritage." Please spend time in Colossians. We put on love, humility, and kindness, and we must put off, over and over those enemies that visit us. Of course, the number one way to destroy patterns of sin is by knowing, memorizing, and wielding the Sword of the Spirit, the Word of God.

Is there a better tool to live in the faith in purity than OBEDIENCE? I have had so much fun with the Greek word obedience; hupakoe,' which means "to be under submission to what is heard." My level of growth in Grace is revealed by the way I obey. So Hebrews 5:8,9 says, though He was a Son, He learned obedience by the things He suffered. And having been perfected, He became the author of eternal salvation to all who obey Him.

Let's build four simple "WAYS" of postures for our life

1. BOW IN HUMILITY.

Ephesians 3:14 says, For this reason, I bow my knees to the Father of our Lord Jesus Christ, from whom the whole family in heaven and earth is named, 17 that Christ may dwell in your hearts through faith; that you, being rooted and grounded in love.

2. STAND-WARFARE

Ephesians 6:10-19 says, Stand, therefore, Put on the full armor of God. 1Peter 1:15 The grass withers, the flowers fade, but the Word of the Lord stands forever. Psalms 33:11 says The counsel of the Lord stands forever, the plans of His heart to all generations.

3. WALK-FAITH

2 Corinthians 5:7 says, For we walk by faith, not sight. Romans 8:1 says, There is therefore now no condemnation to those who are in Christ Jesus, who do not walk according to the flesh, but according to the Spirit

4. RUN-SPIRIT MOVEMENT

John 7:38 says For out of your belly flows (RUNS) Rivers of living water. This river spoken of is the Holy Spirit.

Judges 2:22a says WALK AS THE FATHER'S KEPT THEM: 1. Psalm 68:5–A father of the fatherless, 2. Isaiah 63:16–Father Redeemer from Everlasting is Your name. 3. Isaiah 64:8 But now, O LORD, You are our Father; We are the clay, and You are the potter. 4. Matthew 6:6 pray to your Father who is in the secret place; and your Father who sees in secret will reward you openly. 5. Matthew 6:14-"For if you forgive men their trespasses, your heavenly Father will also forgive you. 6. John 4:23–But the hour is coming, and now is, when the true worshipers will worship the Father in spirit and truth; for the Father is seeking such to worship Him 7. John 14:6–Jesus said to him, "I am the way, the truth, and the life. No one comes to the Father except through Me. 8. John 14:26–But the Helper, the Holy Spirit, whom the Father will send in My name

Prayer- Father, I lay down a pattern of Faith through Purity in me, my family, and my future generations. Galatians proclaim: that I am redeemed from the curse of the law. Poverty, sickness, and death have no place in my life in the name of Jesus. I choose the SECRET of obedience to the Holy Spirit today. AMEN

CHAPTER FOUR
His Desires, My Desires?

Scripture Foundation

Psalms 37:4b-And He shall give you the desires

Proverbs 2:22- (Winning over unfaithfulness) But the wicked will be cut off from the earth, And the unfaithful will be uprooted from it.

SECRET: HOLY DESIRES EQUALS FAITHFUL

Verse 22 is the crescendo of a chapter filled with faith in purity. Scholars had tried to understand when Solomon asked for an understanding heart in 1 Kings 3; why Jehovah was so pleased. The Hebrew will tell us that he asked for the father's desire and discernment. I am convinced that faith must be attached to His desire in us when we ask in faith. This means we must know Him! If I am asking through my desire, the result will be asking amiss (James 4:3). If it is His

THE FAITH IN PURITY

desire in me through a relationship with Him, it will be pure faith.

There are two roads. There are only two ways to live. There are two paths; there are two gates; there are two destinations, and there are two groups of people. They travel on either the broad or narrow road, immoral or blameless, the left or right. So he will find in your tent, hidden or holy, and you will be called faithful or unfaithful in the end.

So, to paraphrase Proverbs chapter 2, ask for wisdom, discernment, and understanding, seek after them as for silver and treasure. The treasure found will be the fear of the Lord. The Lord will deliver from the crooked, perversity, and immoral woman. Immoral ways lead to death! The upright and the blameless will possess the land. So then vs. 22; the wicked will be cut off, and the unfaithful will be uprooted.

"The unfaithful will be uprooted." In Revelations 17, the picture is painted regarding the age's end. The beast, the anti-Christ, is arising; NO ONE CAN DENY THAT. Verse 13-14 says those under the beast give their power and authority to him. 14They will make war with the Lamb, and the Lamb will overcome them. And those who are with Him will be Called, Chosen, and Faithful. WOW!

Jesus painted such incredible pictures when describing the faithful. But, of course, the topic is

Faith and the motive behind it. So, when one was given five talents, another two and another one. It is a gift. It must be used or lost. Matthew 25:24,25 says Then he who had received the one talent came and said, 'Lord, I knew you to be a hard man, reaping where you have not sown, and gathering where you have not scattered seed. And I was afraid and went and hid your talent in the ground. Look, there you have what is yours.' The Lord cannot stand religious jargon. Continue reading, and you will see that this person is not just wrong, but wicked, whose destiny is outer darkness. He cares what you do with what has been given?

If there is no relationship between the gift given and the Giver, "The unfaithful will be uprooted." PLEASE be faithful with what the Lord has given you. Earlier in chapter 25, the gift was oil in the lamp. Anointing from the Holy Spirit, the ability to burn. When the groom comes, YOU MUST BE SELFISH with your oil. You must be selfish with your time in His presence. You must be full of Holy Spirit oil, or the enemy will find a way to sabotage and "cut you off" from His blessing. Of course, He called us His LIGHT!

In Chapter 20 of Matthew, we see the folks being sent out to labor, some in the morning, mid-morning, afternoon, and at quitting time. Our pay is the same in His kingdom, the gift of salvation from Jesus. Please listen; the next level after being

THE FAITH IN PURITY

called is CHOSEN. On that day, your salvation will cost the same, believing that He died and rose. But clearly, the rewards in heaven will vary! There will be two choices—obedience or complaining, called or chosen. Called is defined as "come on in to work'. Chosen is defined as, do your job with honor, integrity, and obedience. I have been guilty of saying, "I've worked all day in the hot sun, and that low life over there just started fifteen minutes ago." OOPS!

Just be FAITHFUL!

Holy Spirit, I pray that my attitude keeps honorable and obedient. Father, I give no power to the spirit of this world or the beast. Spirit, keep my oil burning, let me use all that you have given me, and not be cut off. Let me unlock the secret of holy desires. I can only imagine the moment you say to me, WELL DONE, GOOD AND FAITHFUL SERVANT!!

CHAPTER FIVE
Opening the Gate of Grace

Scripture Foundation

1 Peter 5:8 Be sober, be vigilant; because your adversary the devil walks about like a roaring lion, seeking whom he may devour.

SECRET- GRACE PURSUES HOPE, AND GRACE FOLLOWS FAITH

Joshua 2:21,22

(Winning over pursuers)

Then she said, According to your words, so be it. And she (Rahab) sent them away, and they departed. And she bound the scarlet cord in the window. So they left, went to the mountain, and stayed there three days until the pursuers returned. The pursuers sought them all along the way but did not find them.

Let us first ponder the character Rahab. It seems

that the Father has always been very fond of ladies of the street. The spies divinely spotted her in Jericho, gave her a mission to save His people, and God adopted her to the lineage of Jesus, yes, a distant grandmother to Jesus. And how is it that Rahab would have a "Scarlet Cord."

I'm sure Jesus would remember Rahab when extending a scarlet cord and casting devils out of Mary Magdalene or defending the woman thrown in the street by the hypocrites. Yet, these women received Jesus' secret grace in their life. In our introduction the three hopeless folks pursued and found grace. For these women of the street, GRACE FOUND THEM. They did nothing to merit His grace. They not only did not have faith but should also have been stoned under Moses' law. Rahab's hospitality turned into a salvation miracle for her and Israel. In the woman's case in John 8, she was thrown in the street and publicly shamed. Oh, the scarlet cord of Grace that wrapped around that woman on the street. The law, her sin, and my sin melting under the incredible SECRET favor. Religious big mouths with the stones walked away, and redemption was there to stay!

Faith can come after you have pursued pure hope and landed in desperation. But, let not your heart grow weary because great faith will prevail if you do not grow weary. Luke 18:1 says, Don't ever give up praying. The miracle for your loved one or friend might be today!

Women were "lesser" in Hebrew culture. Jesus changed it all with grace. Understanding the context is essential to see the significance that was taking place in John 4 when Jesus met the adulteress at the well. Jesus was not supposed to talk to Samaritans. Grace was screaming, I don't care who you are, I want to make you a fountain instead of a dam, and I want to turn it into a river. Hallelujah!

Thank you, Jesus, for the Scarlet cord that flows from Moses to Abraham, from Noah to David, and the offspring of David keep flowing until the ultimate scarlet blood would flow to you and me.

1 Peter 5:8, 9 instructs us about your adversary, the devil who walks about like a roaring lion, seeking whom he may devour. Resist him, steadfast in the faith, knowing that the same sufferings are experienced by your brotherhood in the world.

Fear will intimidate. As courage comes and the noise screams, it is only a toothless lion speaking with a megaphone. At times we must pursue and defeat our enemy, and at times, the Holy Spirit will direct us into hiding, into HIS SECURE STRONGHOLD.

Psalm 61:3,4 says For You have been a shelter for me, a strong tower from the enemy. I will abide in Your tabernacle forever; I will trust in the shelter of

Your wings.

Josh 2:22-The pursuers sought them all along the way but did not find them. Just as Jericho (a stronghold of false religion) would be destroyed, we must destroy all false gods and every appearance of evil in our lives and homes. And understand that wrong passionate desires will follow you, hound you, search for you. Father will find you in your place, wrap His scarlet cloak around you, and redeem you.

Father, in Jesus' name, we walk in obedience around any strongholds in our lives. We blow the trumpet over Jericho, declaring the God of Abraham will destroy all barriers to freedom. Thank you for pursuing me in my hopeless place. We extend a scarlet cord and the blood of Jesus to all family members. Our enemy is Satan, and he will pursue us until Jesus throws him in the lake of fire. We resist him in Jesus' name, and he will flee. In Christ name, AMEN

CHAPTER SIX
THE HOLY SPIRIT VS PRETENSE

SCRIPTURE FOUNDATION

PSALM 50:2 SO OUT OF ZION, THE PERFECTION OF BEAUTY, GOD WILL SHINE FORTH.

SECRET: M+C+C+C—2+2 = FAITH

Esther 2:19-23 (Winning over obstacles to our destiny) When virgins were gathered together a second time, Mordecai sat within the king's gate. Now Esther had not revealed her family and her people, just as Mordecai had charged her, for Esther obeyed the command of Mordecai when he brought her up. In those days, while Mordecai sat within the king's gate, two of the king's eunuchs, Bigthan and Teresh, doorkeepers, became furious and sought to lay hands on King Ahasuerus. So, the matter became known to Mordecai, who told Queen Esther, and Esther informed the king in Mordecai's name. And when an inquiry was made into the issue, it was confirmed. Both were hanged on gallows, and it was written in the book of the chronicles in the king's presence.

Oh, what joy to unveil this hallmark story and discover "the faith in purity" again. Let's use some symbolism as we unfold the story. Mordecai is (Holy Spirit), Bigthan and Teresh is (fear and shame) Hamen is (pretense) and Esther is (You and I). In the end, the gallows for three villains were symbolic of judgment. God is the Judge. The ultimate question is, what caused Esther to approach the king IN FAITH with death pending with 10's of thousands of Jews' lives at stake? Where was this faith born? We find a woman with no parents, (orphaned), who was born with a purpose of prophetic beauty and deliverance. Please reflect that no matter where you come from, or your status, the Holy Spirit will adopt you and train you to have faith. It is clear several times in this passage that Esther would undoubtedly listen to Mordecai (Holy Spirit) and obey his instruction. To follow under authority will always be the foundation of strong faith. So, the Holy Spirit takes in Esther and becomes her father, teacher, and advocate.

We find 2:22 in the story where Bigthan & Teresh (Fear and Shame) were about to sabotage Father's entire plan. Hamen (pretense) was behind their plot. Fear and shame are ruthless, relentless, and want you to die. Instead, they were hung on the gallows they built. The story would later end with Esther's incredible approach to the king. The man with the hidden agenda, Hamen, was plotting to do away with the Holy Spirit. It is the glory of the king to uncover secrets, Proverbs 25:2. In the middle of the night, the King remembered Mordecai, who saved him from Bigthan & Teresh. The plot would be discovered, and through Esther, PRETENSE (HAMEN) was hanged on the gallows built for Mordecai (Holy Spirit). WOW!

A significant key to this story and pure faith is the preparation that was given to Esther. This preparation is in tandem with the Loving care of the Holy Spirit (Mordecai) to Esther. Esther 2:12b says the days of their preparation apportioned: six months with oil of myrrh and six months with perfumes and preparations for beautifying women. In Exodus 30:24, we see the ingredients of anointing oil. They are Myrrh, cinnamon, calamus, and cassia. Two plus two, four legs of solid faith. Esther was anointed for twelve months to come before the King.

This orphaned nobody, received and nurtured by the Holy Spirit, was chosen above all in the kingdom to be Queen and deliver her people. He will accept us as beggars, orphans, sinners, murderers, hypocrites, etc. YOU ARE CALLED and must answer the call! But the CHOSEN anointing will take some preparation. The preparation and sacrifice looked like this: Myrrh-Meekness, (posture-yielding your rights) Cinnamon-uprightness (how you stand) Calamus- (Sweet Flag) Sweet Aroma to the Father-When ripe, it drops to the ground-humility. Cassia- (Aroma, stripped of pride). Pure faith is meekness, uprightness, humility, and stripped of pride! To conclude, let's define beauty, according to Prov. 31:30 Charm is deceitful, and beauty is passing, but a woman who fears the Lord shall be praised. Beautiful is, Fearing the Lord. Psalms. Ps. 50:2- So out of Zion, the perfection of beauty, God will shine forth. We are the vessels to shine forth His beauty. Faith and purity came by the Holy Spirit through the lavish preparation ordered by Father God.

Father, as a member of the Bride of Christ, I submit myself to your preparation, humility, and meekness. I send fear and shame to the gallows. Pretense must be exposed, and go there too. I choose the preparation of meekness and humility. I submit to you for my prophetic purpose for my life. In Jesus name, Amen.

CHAPTER SEVEN
Uncovering All Pride

Scripture Foundation

Psalm 51:1b Blot out my transgressions. Wash me thoroughly from my iniquity, and cleanse me from my sin.

SECRET: PRIDE'S PRETTY FOUNDATION WILL CRUMBLE

Jeremiah 2: 22 (Winning over pride) For though you wash yourself with lye and use much soap, Yet your iniquity is marked before Me," says the Lord GOD.

What a segway from the humble preparation, anointing of Esther to a chapter full of pride. The 2:22 summation of this chapter tries to scrub with lye soap, and it cannot be cleansed. Allow me to paraphrase the first twenty-one verses of Jeremiah 2 with 22 items in a paragraph.

THE FAITH IN PURITY

1. You left your first love. 2. You trashed your tithe, 3-disaster will come upon you 4- you've gone after idols. 5-I gave you a bountiful land, and you defiled it. 6-The pastors did not know me 7-prophets trusted Baal. 8-This will affect your children and Grandchildren. 9-you have exchanged glory for what is not profitable. 10- you have forsaken living waters. 11-you have hewn broken cisterns with no water. 12-You've been made a slave 13-Your land is a waste, 14-Your city burned. 15-The crown of your head is broken 16-The fear of the Lord is not in you, 17-Your wickedness will rebuke you 18-Your backsliding will correct you 19-I have broken your yoke,20- I have burst your bonds,21- You have played the harlot 22- You have turned a high-quality plant into a degenerate plant.

Then verse 22, You attempt to wash with lye, but your iniquity remains. The prophet is on a roll describing Israel's tragic downfall. Remember Mordecai and his discovery of the enemy's plot. So get out the humble oils and the perfumes and get anointed and Spirit beautiful! The battle we are fighting against is PRIDE.

Out of all those descriptions, let's highlight 2: 1st, "the crown of your head is broken." I believe this could mean both the crown of your head and the crown on your head. The Crown represents royalty, authority, and power. My friends, the crux of the matter is that Father wants you to be a king and a priest unto your God. Revelation 1:6 says You cannot have strong faith if you don't humble yourself, and then take authority over your enemies. 2nd, the fear of the Lord is not in you. When I sin, I ignore, undermine, and resist the Spirit that lives inside of me. I have taken on the identity of pretense. But our goal is the fear of the Lord, the beginning of wisdom and knowledge.

    Let's break down pride. Please dig deeper into each word to destroy these enemies. PRIDE: fixed on your dignity and confidence. Antonym: humility. PRETENSE: insincere behavior, intention to deceive, unwarranted behavior. Antonym: purity. INDEPENDENCE: Doing things on your own. Antonym: meekness. CONCEIT: pride multiplied. Antonym: contrite. SELFISHNESS: not considering others, absorbed in yourself. Antonym: broken

    Our text is telling us that Father wants to be first. It doesn't work if we try to wash with the best soap. PRIDE MUST GO!

    Holy Spirit, let me destroy all lords that are not You. Let me destroy pretense and secret sins. I cannot cleanse myself with good works or good deeds. I have the royal blood of King Jesus. He sees me white as snow through Christ's blood. In Christ Name, I confess the sin of pride, and He is faithful and just to forgive. According to Rom 11, I am grafted into Jesus the True Vine. Father, the crown that you have placed on my head, I cast at your feet. I cannot have a life apart from YOU. In Christ Name AMEN

CHAPTER EIGHT
Deep Secrets, or Secret Sins

Scripture Foundation

1 Corinthians 1:7 But we speak the wisdom of God in a mystery, the hidden wisdom which God ordained before the ages for our glory.

Daniel 2:22 (Winning over secret sins) He reveals deep and secret things; He knows what is in the darkness, and light dwells with Him.

SECRET: KNOWING FATHER CREATES SEEING EYES

We are exposing pretense, the secret place of pride. Daniel shows us that when the Holy Spirit takes our appetite, incredible knowledge and secrets will be revealed by the Father. In God's Word, a favorite study for me is secrets, treasures, and mysteries. He has created us to search and discover. In a world of knowledge, the internet, distraction has taken away the discovery of knowledge. Finding treasure has become instant by google. May our love for Father bring us to dig deep into the treasures of the WORD OF GOD.

One topic we have not addressed in this discovery is "fasting." Could you deny that Daniel is the best example of faith and purity in the Bible? Too bad the bible doesn't reveal his parents and childhood, where did he learn the prayer and fasting culture? He begins his pure journey by rejecting the Golden Corral buffet in the king's court, risking his life (by disobeying the king's rules.) Instead, he chose the salad bar. "OUCH"! Think about your life. On a scale of 1-10, what has been the total INFLUENCE and effect of FOOD in your life? Well, there is no better way to faith and purity than to kill your flesh through fasting. Not just food, but pleasantries such as TV, desserts, and hobbies that you love. The father wants me to have all those pleasantries, but oh, do they taste better when sacrificing them for a while. It's about me having control over those things. Let's define it in 2 words, gluttony and moderation, OUCH!!

Oh, the evils that can come on Facebook, of course is a huge blessing to me. I enjoy videos of deer and elk coming into a blind. Or the most incredible college and pro, last-second miracles, and plays. Yes, Christian comedians, singers, and tears as the most influential songs are playing on facebook and youtube. Only to scroll down and be defiled, lured, and assaulted by fleshly carnage. Oh, it makes me mad, and I have not always won that battle. Middle agers, many elderly have never fought this battle because they don't use Facebook. You say, "it's not pornography!" That's debatable, but in short, abstain from all appearances of evil 1 Thessalonians. 5:22. You can't mix spiritual and earthly things. I Thessalonians 4:4,5a simply says that each of you should know how to possess his vessel in sanctification and honor, not in passionate lust.

Look at anyone you know who is Godly with great character and knows how to die to the flesh. Daniel 2:22, knowing the Father will result in the revealing of His deep secrets. Meekness is defined as "yielding up my rights." So, if you need to break a stronghold, fast cherished things!! I was so thankful when I asked the Lord to purify my heart, and it showed up on my clock at 2:22.

When Jesus told a story, they all kept saying, Jesus, why do you talk in riddles? "Because My kingdom is based on faith." Faith comes by hearing and uncovering the mystery of who He is, not by Google. Revelation will come one Word at a time, line upon line, precept by precept. Matthew 5:6 says Pure Hunger will be the path to righteousness. Jesus, let this be said of me; Daniel 5:12 Inasmuch as an excellent spirit, knowledge, understanding, interpreting dreams, solving riddles, and explaining enigmas were found in this Daniel. Read Esther 4:16- She and all her staff fasted and prayed before she walked down that aisle to approach the king. Matt 6:1a-When you fast. Not if! Is. 58:6a-This is the fast, to loosen chains, and untie chords. Lord, may a Daniel spirit in me reveal seeing eyes.

Lord, I set my heart to be as Daniel and pray fervently and fast. Lord, teach me how to fast to increase my hunger for Your Word. Teach me to find secrets, treasures, and mysteries in your Word. Lord, reveal deep things in me that are not pleasing to you. I release them to you. In Jesus name Amen

CHAPTER NINE
Grace, Grace, Grace - He's Coming Soon

Scripture Foundation

MATTHEW 24:36 BUT OF THAT DAY AND HOUR NO ONE KNOWS, NOT EVEN THE ANGELS OF HEAVEN, BUT MY FATHER ONLY.

SECRET: GRAIN, OIL, WINE IN YOU

JOEL 2:22-23 Do not be afraid, you beasts of the field; for the open pastures are springing up, and the tree bears its fruit; For He has given you the former rain faithfully, and He will cause the rain to come down for you, the former rain, and the latter rain in the first month.

You may have noticed I love the topic of GRACE, and divinely, here it is again. In Joel chapter 2, we are about to get a vision of THE LAW TURNING INTO GRACE. This chapter's prophetic and apocalyptic (unveiling) visions are genuinely astounding.

In this passage and surrounding, we see three key points 1. Do not be afraid, 2. The former rain, and the latter rain in the first month. 3. The threshing floors shall be full of wheat, and the vats shall overflow with new wine and oil.

I remember a moment, maybe ten or eleven years old, when I saw a movie that unveiled what it might look like in the end times. On the way home, I still remember HWY 14, looking out of the car into the sky with tears rolling down my face. In short, the government controls every part of us. Well, here we are. It is not even hidden anymore. It is blatant and in your face. So, our passage reveals to not fear and that the former and the latter rain will be upon us. When he comes, will your garment be white? This unveiling will be revealed through three elements, vs. 19:

THE GRAIN - THE GRACE OF THE END TIME HARVEST. Jesus said, the fields are white unto harvest. We must all do our part to present the grain offering. Share the good news with all those in your town and those outside your town. Obey, and He will bless you abundantly. You will be judged by what you did or did not do. According to Matthew 25, you will be one of two things: a sheep on the right or a goat on the left. Vs. 41 says of those goats on the left, you will have your place in everlasting fire prepared for the devil and his angels.

OIL - REPRESENTS THE GRACE OF REVELATION and HUMILITY as we have seen from Esther. But borrowing someone else's oil does not work. Is your revelation oil pure and full? Is your lamp of expectation and hope burning? He is coming for a pure bride! So then, when the midnight cry occurs, we will be known by either a vessel having oil or those that do not. And the chariot will sweep the burning ones away, and for some, weeping and gnashing of teeth.

WINE - REPRESENTS THE GRACE OF ANOINTING of the Holy Spirit upon God's Word- At the wedding in Cana, there stood six waterpots for His miracle, usually made of clay, but these were made of stone. So new Wine begins on the foundation of Jesus the Chief Cornerstone. This wine would not be mixed with human clay but of pure stone. So, 1 Corinthians 3:12,13 says, Now if anyone builds on this foundation with gold, silver, precious stones, wood, hay, straw, each one's work will become evident; for the Day will declare it because it will be revealed by fire.

As we live our lives tried by fire in Christ, we will have two choices. One is to be charred because our foundation is wood, hay, or stubble, or the second is to be refined as gold, hewn into silver vessels unto honor, and stone pots which Jesus would make into New Wine.

THE FAITH IN PURITY

Lord Jesus, MARANATHA, "come quickly." And as the day draws near, may my grain be full. May I lead many to Christ. Lord, may I be filled with your oil of revelation and understanding. When you arrive, may I be drunk and burning with the fire of the Holy Spirit. A pure vessel, full of New Wine. In Christ Name, AMEN!

CHAPTER TEN
The Gift Of Resolve (Part 1)

Scripture Foundation

Matthew 5:37-But let your 'Yes' be 'Yes,' and your 'No,' 'No.'

SECRET: THE WORD CREATES ABSOLUTES, CREATES PURITY, CREATES FAITH

Mark 2:22 - (Winning over the spirit of religion) And no one puts new wine into old wineskins; or else the new wine bursts the wineskins, the wine is spilled, and the wineskins are ruined. But new wine must be put into new wineskins.

Pharisees and Sadducees were great Old Testament scholars. But, oh, did Jesus make them mad. The new Kingdom would be about grace, and the old law remembered, but a shadow! They were settled into the old covenant, and their tough old wineskins could not handle Holy Spirit water and fire. Jesus symbolized this in Cana. Those waterpots of purification became the best wine ever. He made water into wine. He made blind eyes open. He made the lame walk and the dumb talk. I am glad that, again, 2:22 brings us to the religious spirit.

Moses and Elijah and Elisha did miracles. What kind of wine was that? The type of wine that only rested on prophets, priests, kings. The anointing came upon them, it was not in them. Jesus' kingdom would begin with Him showing us the Father. Jesus' exit plan was to fill up every willing vessel with new wine in the upper room in fifty days, and clearly, this pouring out has not ceased. For those who believe that it has ended, well I'll just say, heaven will reveal one day a big surprise to you.

The works that He did, we must do, and even greater! Here are two Faith in purity goals.

1. Revelation 1:6 Be a King and Priest unto your God.

2. 1 Corinthians 14:1 Desire the best gift, but especially that you may prophesy.

My job is to push you and give you goals. Please assess your wineskin. This study is to make your vessel fit for new wine! To expose the surface of your wineskin and get a new one. To make your vessel fit for His potency. New wine will destroy religious bigotry and pride, shame and fear, and condemnation.

An excellent study of a significant word is the word "resolve." That word is not in many scriptures, but resolve defines doing instead of talking. It defines a mature, YES, or NO. Consider this before David slew Goliath: David said, "Is there not a cause?" Where is the RESOLVE IN THIS SITUATION? Resolve can define the answer for our culture, families, and government.

RESOLVE - to deal with successfully: clear up, with incredible resolve. Abraham had one of the most challenging decisions ever. But, in short, his resolve to keep his mouth shut and simply obey Jehovah's command to slay his son. What a critical moment in our history. The covenant of faith began at this RESOLVE to trust Jehovah no matter what.

RESOLVE- to declare or decide by a formal resolution. Everyone loves Peter. In Acts 11, his old wineskin was about to burst, and the Holy Spirit, through a dream, would reveal that the gospel would also come even to the pathetic, dirty gentiles. Remember the pork chops coming from heaven. For those who don't understand, Jews could not eat unclean things. Then we come to Acts 11:23, which says, ``When he arrived and saw the grace of God, he was glad and encouraged all of them to remain faithful to the Lord with a firm resolve of the heart." This resolve, my friends, allowed you and me gentiles to receive the gospel.

RESOLVE -To reach a firm decision about. The arrival in heaven of the dear saint named Stephen must have been grand. He knew when he preached that death was probable. But with great RESOLVE, HE SPOKE in Acts 6:13. Every member of the supreme council focused his gaze on Stephen, for right in front of their eyes, while being falsely accused, his face glowed as though he had the face of an angel! Acts 7:55,60 says But Stephen, overtaken with great faith, was full of the Holy Spirit. He fixed his gaze into the heavenly realm and saw the glory and splendor of God—and Jesus, who stood up at the right hand of God. "Look!" Stephen said. "I can see the heavens opening and the Son of Man standing at the right hand of God to welcome me home!" He crumpled to his knees and shouted in a loud voice, "Our Lord, don't hold this sin against them." And then he died."

Holy Spirit, give me a new wineskin to take your new wine. I desire the gift of prophecy. I desire faith like Abraham, Obedience like Peter, and boldness like Stephen, and allow me to set my face like Stephen to give my life even unto death. I resolve to succeed in my decisions and have strong faith to the end. In Christ name, AMEN

CHAPTER ELEVEN
The Gift Of Resolve (Part 2)

Scripture Foundation

Proverbs 3:5-Trust in the Lord with all your heart

Mark 2:22-(when faith becomes TRUST) And no one puts new wine into old wineskins; or else the new wine bursts the wineskins, the wine is spilled, and the wineskins are ruined. But new wine must be put into new wineskins.

SECRET: CLEAN FOUNTAINS OF FAITH, PURE RIVERS OF TRUST-TRUST GROWS FROM FAITH

RESOLVE- to resolve doubts

I love history, and I love stories. The following paints an incredible picture of the resolve in faith, and takes us to another level of faith; TRUST. Trust is the acting verb past FAITH. Your level of

THE FAITH IN PURITY

PURITY will definitely influence TRUST.

The story of Charles Blondin and Harry Colcord provides a great illustration. Blondin was the foremost tightrope walker of his time. He gained worldwide fame in 1859 as the first person to cross Niagara Falls. Colcord was his friend and manager. A cable made entirely of hemp, 1,300 feet long and two inches in diameter, was wound around an oak tree on the American side, while the other end was ferried across the Niagara River and secured to a Canadian rock. To limit swaying, Colcord had stabilizing ropes affixed at 20-foot intervals to anchors on both banks—except for 50 unreachable feet in the center, which sagged and swayed dangerously. Thanks to Colcord's savvy marketing, tens of thousands of spectators gathered for the spectacle. Gamblers took bets on whether Blondin would fall and die or survive. Shortly before 5:00 p.m. on June 30, 1859, Blondin started his slow walk from the American side.

Once past the center section, he broke into a run! After a brief rest, he started back again, but this time toting a box camera on his back. Balancing precariously near the middle, Blondin carefully set up the camera and snapped a picture of the crowd. Then he repacked his burden and continued the rest of the way. The entire round trip took 23 minutes. Once safely back on American soil, Blondin immediately announced a series of encore performances, each more daring than the last. The press ate it up. Over several weeks, Blondin walked backward, blindfolded, backflipped, pushed a wheelbarrow, and even cooked an omelet during one of many trips across the rope. The spectators, on the other hand, only had faith—a difference seen in Blondin's daring walk in August 1859. After he had crossed to the Canadian side, the crowd was horrified as Blondin reappeared on the rope with his manager, Harry Colcord, clinging to his back. A few guy ropes snapped during their transit, but Blondin never wavered and safely made the crossing. It was later reported that Blondin told his manager, "Look up, Harry…you are no longer Colcord, you are Blondin. Until I finish this walk, be a part of me, mind, body, and soul. If I sway, sway with me. Do not attempt to do any balancing yourself." This is the difference between faith and trust. The spectators had faith in Blondin and believed in his abilities. But only Colcord trusted him enough to climb on his back and allow him to carry him across.

With great resolve, we must climb on the back of Jesus, and hang on and trust. Mark 11:23-24. "For assuredly, I say to you, whoever says to this mountain, 'Be removed and be cast into the sea,' and does not doubt in his heart, but believes that those things he says will be done, he will have whatever he says.

Father, I choose to obey what you say, no matter how difficult it may be. Jesus, I hold on to you, and I ask you to be my guide, be my legs, be my vision. Holy Spirit, I choose to listen to your voice, I am your child. In Christ name, AMEN

CHAPTER TWELVE
THE GIFT OF RESOLVE (PART 3)

SCRIPTURE FOUNDATION

ROMANS 8:28a- FOR THOSE WHO LOVE GOD, ALL THINGS WORK TOGETHER FOR GOOD.

MARK 2:22- AND NO ONE PUTS NEW WINE INTO OLD WINESKINS; OR ELSE THE NEW WINE BURSTS THE WINESKINS, THE WINE IS SPILLED, AND THE WINESKINS ARE RUINED. BUT NEW WINE MUST BE PUT INTO NEW WINESKINS.

RESOLVE- To resolve a dispute, to resolve the problem into simple elements- to find an answer to make clear or understandable

SECRET: BEHOLD, I MAKE ALL THINGS NEW "A ROAD IN THE WILDERNESS AND RIVERS IN THE DESERT." ISAIAH 43:19(PARAPHRASE)

In a world in which evil is rampant, death and tragedy, and tyranny is abounding, there must be a resolve in us that "His will be done." GOD IS GOOD, HE DID NOT DEVISE EVIL, CANNOT DO EVIL, BUT HE HAS A PLAN, AND WE MUST FIGHT, AND WATCH AND PRAY. May my wineskin be filled with new hope, and faith and trust as I fill out my days.

PEARL HARBOR- Sunday, December 7th, 1941— Admiral Chester Nimitz was attending a concert in Washington, DC. He was paged and told there was a phone call for him. When he answered the phone, it was President Franklin Delano Roosevelt on the phone. He told Admiral Nimitz that he (Nimitz) would now be the Commander of the Pacific Fleet. Admiral Nimitz flew to Hawaii to assume command of the Pacific Fleet. He landed at Pearl Harbor on Christmas Eve, 1941. There was such a spirit of despair, dejection and defeat-- you would have thought the Japanese had already won the war. On Christmas Day, 1941, Adm. Nimitz was given a boat tour of the destruction wrought on Pearl Harbor by the Japanese. Big sunken battleships and navy vessels cluttered the waters everywhere you looked. As the tour boat returned to dock, the young helmsman of the boat asked, "Well Admiral, what do you think after seeing all this destruction?" Admiral Nimitz's reply shocked everyone within the sound of his voice. Admiral Nimitz said, "The Japanese made three of the biggest mistakes an attack force could ever make, or God was taking care of America. Which do you think it was?" Shocked and surprised, the young helmsman asked, "What do you mean by saying the Japanese made the three biggest mistakes an attack force ever made? Nimitz explained: Mistake number one: The Japanese attacked on Sunday morning. Nine out of every ten crewmen of those ships were ashore on leave. If those same ships had been lured to sea and been sunk--we would have lost 38,000 men instead of 3,800. Mistake number two: When the Japanese saw all those battleships lined in a row, they got so carried away sinking those battleships, they never once bombed our dry docks opposite those ships. If they had destroyed our dry docks, we would have had to tow every one of those ships to America to be repaired. As it is now, the ships are in shallow water and can be raised. One tug can pull them over to the dry docks, and we can have them repaired and at sea by the time we could have towed them to America. And I already have crews ashore anxious to man those ships. Mistake number three: Every drop of fuel in the Pacific theater of war is on top of the ground storage tanks five miles away over that hill. One attack plane could have strafed those tanks and destroyed our fuel supply.

I resolve that no matter how bad things look, Admiral Jesus sees the big picture, and that my finite mind must allow Him to fulfill His plan.

Holy Spirit, let my life be spilling over with your prophetic fullness. Thank you for the old traditions of my lineage, but I want the new wine. I will talk to you Admiral Jesus when I can't see your purpose. Baptize me in the Holy Spirit. Fill me with knowledge, wisdom, prophecy, fruits, and gifts straight from the Holy Spirit. Use them Lord as tools to make me pure, and therefore increase my faith. In Christ name, AMEN

CHAPTER THIRTEEN
Go To The Ant You Sluggard

Scripture Foundation

Luke 2:22—(Winning over Laziness) Now when the days of her purification according to the law of Moses were completed, they brought Him to Jerusalem to present Him to the Lord

2 Timothy 2:15-Be diligent to present yourself approved to God, a worker who does not need to be ashamed, rightly dividing the word of truth.

SECRET: PROVERBS 13:5b TPT WHAT A WASTE WHEN AN INCOMPETENT SON SLEEPS THROUGH HIS DAY OF OPPORTUNITY

According to Jewish tradition, women after childbirth, when the child was a boy, were unclean for seven days, and then had to stay at home thirty-three days more (at the birth of a girl these periods were doubled). Then they were bound to present in the temple an offering of purification. This journey to trust starts with being approved to God, disciplined, longsuffering, and studying, and doing necessary things to renew your mind.

When the veil was torn, the wineskin of grace began replacing law. But Jewish people still did Jewish rituals. A favorite passage of mine, Heb 13:15 says By Him therefore let us offer up a sacrifice of praise to God continually, that is the fruit of our lips giving thanks to His name. Don't know about you, but, disciplining myself in sacrifice, and study, and memory, and thanksgiving does not come easy for me. There is a book that helped me in my 20's by Richard Foster called the Celebration of Discipline. In short, he covers the disciplines of prayer, and solitude, and fasting, and study, and simplicity etc… Just those five alone make me say "ouch". How many folks really have a powerful prayer and devotional life? What if every Christian did? Oh, would the church be a powerful force! Yes, this book is about passion and desire for the Word. Set your face, my friend, to fast, and pray, and get rid of laziness.

Lord, we ask you to help us to live a daily life and while dying to the flesh, let us memorize God's

Word, and wean ourselves from milk, and desire spiritual meat. (Heb 5:13) As proverbs remind us, let us not be a sluggard, and lazy, but diligent.

THE CAMELEON AND THE ANT

by Tim Pomp

A Chameleon passed by an ant one day, and said, come on stop working, it's time to play.

You and your co-ants are building your life, while I sit on my branch, no stress, no strife.

But my life is lonely and I'm tired of rest, when ants wiz by I admit they are the best.

When one needs volunteers, I simply turn gray, but I'm bored and angry and tired most days.

When pressure gets tough, I turn red and blue, I pose and turn a clown, I know what to do.

I'm always afraid, my façade soon will be, a pathetic meaningless blob on the branch of this tree.

So as I lay myself down on my perch every night, my multiple colors well they just don't seem right

I have real big words, big plans, but I cry, help me, please to win, Mr. Ant before I die.

To begin Mr. Ant said, I must work real, real hard, Creator made me really small, but put me in charge.

From the lowest Ant to the five Star Ant General, each one is a servAnt, sufficient and able.

THE FAITH IN PURITY

Though the smallest of creatures, I have no excuse, with teamwork, and wisdom, we absolutely refuse.

To worry, cause strife, and let fear invade, like "little David, though small I will giants slay.

But above all, oh Chameleon my colorful friend, I will make things clear, the pathway to win.

The foundation of your life, the wobbly branch of King Me, trust your designer, Creator, He only will make you free.

He'll take your black and gray, yes the color of your sin, and with His brilliant Red, make you white within.

God made you camouflage, to keep enemy away, kick out the lazy, and start working hard today.

For your beautiful yellow, green, brown and tan and blue was given by the Creator: trust in the Lord with all your heart, you'll know what to do!

CHAPTER FOURTEEN
Adultery

Scripture Foundation

Romans 2:22 -(Winning over fornication and adultery)You who say, "Do not commit adultery," do you commit adultery? You who abhor idols, do you rob temples?

Revelation 21:8-But the cowardly, unbelieving, abominable, murderers, sexually immoral, sorcerers, idolaters, and all liars shall have their part in the lake which burns with fire.

SECRET: COME ON, OPEN THOSE DOORS DEEP IN YOUR BEING, SPIRIT WILL SHOW YOU IDOLS

Call it coincidence or anything you want but tell me that it is not amazing that this verse is 2:22. Let's take a minute and define idolatry! Why is it the first command? ``Thou shalt have no other God's before Me". And then thou shalt not commit adultery. It is so simple; the Lord wants to be first. Then when He establishes your life up with a companion, "like a goose" be faithful for the rest of your life. Any other standard is a choice to mess up God's plan. Before you are married, you must have self-control. And as Jesus introduced the new wine of grace and conviction: he said, looking at a woman with wrong passion is to commit fornication Matt. 5:28. Grace defines the New Covenant: His influence, His favor to help you stay pure until marriage and through it.

I will never forget a story from my first youth pastorate. I had about 15 kids to start with in an awesome church in Wyoming with an awesome pastor. After about 2 weeks I needed to make a big decision. After the youth group, like 6 out of the 15 were discovered in secret places making out. So, I decided to firmly declare that we will have standards of purity. I thought my teaching went quite well except after about a month my wonderful youth group went from about 15 youth to 5.

My pastor stood behind my decision, and Hallelujah in time we would grow, and 8-10 years later we would be taking 70+ kids & leaders to our regional conference. Somewhere after these years came the principle of "The Faith in Purity".

One story that defines the battle with these

teens for purity. A gal stood up in the middle of the youth group and stuck her finger at me and said something like; "I can kiss and make-out if I want, no one can stop me". I'm strong enough in my faith, and it doesn't matter if I make out. Well, the discussion was on! This again would define an important place for me, defining faith in Purity. I walked up close to her and said, "thank you for your honesty. My friend this is not my opinion, what I am teaching is the Word of God". Flee youthful lust, abstain from all appearance of evil. To look upon a woman (or man) with wrong intentions is fornication, let alone kissing and making out. This will be the standard here in this place, and that is final." She stormed out of the room. The timetable may be a bit wrong, but I believe it was 3-4 months, and she was pregnant. It was 2+ years from that fateful moment that she boldly defended her flesh, she had 2 children and no young man whatsoever to hold, cherish, and enjoy with. She was another statistic of a single mom. So, what would have happened if through brokenness, she would have submitted to the Word, and to the authority in the church? Much different story!

"Then the LORD saw that the wickedness of man was great in the earth, and that every intent of the thoughts of his heart was only evil continually."— Genesis 6:5

THE FAITH IN PURITY

A radio-cast by David Jeremiah revealed this: January 2016 the largest online porn site unleashed its annual statistics: on this one web site— in the Year 2015 consumers watched——4 billion 392 million 486 thousand 500 hours of porn on their website. By converting these hours into years, in the one year of 2015, people spent over 500,000 years watching porn on this one website.

Romans 2:5-6, 16 "But in accordance with your hardness and your impenitent heart you are treasuring up for yourself wrath in the day of wrath and revelation of the righteous judgment of God, who "will render to each one according to his deeds": in the day when God will judge the secrets of men by Jesus Christ, according to my gospel." If it is not shouting clearly at you o generation, porn is sin, and according to Jesus, fornication. And fornicators will not inherit the Kingdom of Heaven. Rev. 21:8

Holy Spirit, I stand strong against any form of adultery or fornication. I ask you to guard my heart, for out of it flows the issues of life. Keep me pure, Father, so that I can have strong faith. In Christ name, AMEN

CHAPTER FIFTEEN
The Baptism of the Holy Spirit (Part 1)

SCRIPTURE FOUNDATION

PSALM 91:9 BECAUSE YOU HAVE MADE THE LORD, WHO IS MY REFUGE, EVEN THE MOST HIGH YOUR DWELLING PLACE.

EPHESIANS 2:20-22 HAVING BEEN BUILT ON THE FOUNDATION OF THE APOSTLES AND PROPHETS, JESUS CHRIST HIMSELF BEING THE CHIEF CORNERSTONE, 21/ IN WHOM THE WHOLE BUILDING, BEING FITTED TOGETHER, GROWS INTO A HOLY TEMPLE IN THE LORD, 22/ IN WHOM YOU ALSO ARE BEING BUILT TOGETHER FOR A DWELLING PLACE OF GOD IN THE SPIRIT.

SECRET: HUNGER WILL CAUSE THE DAMN TO BREAK AND THE RIVER FLOW

You think it is tough to live as a Christian? I often think of each person in the Old Testament who tried to please Jehovah. Imagine 10 kinds of sacrifice with 10 kinds of sin. What a glorious moment when the Messiah arrived on the scene. Imagine that DOOR, the historic moment when God's grace could live inside a human vessel which arrived on the day of Pentecost. Jesus said, I am the door, symbolizing intimacy. Go through that door, and there will be the Holy Spirit. The wonder of hosting the God of the universe. Heb 11:6 Without faith it is impossible to please God. Faith is who He is, Love is who He is. His plan was to have his presence, his faith, and his love, as in the garden. The purpose overall, to bring as many to His kingdom as possible. We must remind ourselves that His perfect presence lives within us. He is pure, He is perfect, He is faith, and He dwells in us. Wow!

Why am I passionate about the Holy Spirit? I have incredible stories of the enemy's plot to poison people regarding who the Holy Spirit really is. Here is the issue. Do not grieve and quench the Holy Spirit. Pursue Him, and receive His fountain, His river, and His fire. How you do it is not my business, just do it. Hunger is the Key. If you want to ask a person who is on fire, or gushing like a river, I like that idea. But my experience is that religion, and circumstances, and the devil himself will do anything and everything to talk you away from pursuing the FULLNESS OF THE SPIRIT. Also, rivers and fire of the Holy Spirit do not usually live in churches, many churches won't go there! I am sorry about that.

Later, I will share my story about my Goliath, and a visit from the Holy Spirit to forgive. Well, soon after that would be one of the most powerful moments in my life. Please put aside anything you've heard about the Holy Spirit and consider that He wants to dwell in you. Again, it will be your choice what that looks like, a fountain, or a river, or a fire. Oh, the wonderful Word of God- Act 19:1b-6-And finding some disciples he said to them, "Did you receive the Holy Spirit when you believed?" So they said to him, "We have not so much as heard whether there is a Holy Spirit." And he said to them, "Into what then were you baptized?" So they said, "Into John's baptism." Then Paul said, "John indeed baptized with a baptism of repentance, saying to the people that they should believe in Him who would come after him, that is, on Christ Jesus." When they heard this, they were baptized in the name of the Lord Jesus. And when Paul had laid hands on them, the Holy Spirit came upon them, and they spoke with tongues and prophesied.

John 6:44-The Father draws you to Jesus. Jesus leads you to the Holy Spirit. I am so sorry if a leader or pastor doesn't ever talk about this, but nothing in the word is clearer. Jesus had to leave the earth, hallelujah, and leave the best plan in History. You must go through a DOOR CALLED

JESUS. Believe that He died on the cross and rose from the dead, and He will baptize you in the Holy Spirit, to be a fountain (John 4), a river (John 7), and a fire (Matthew 3:11, IF YOU DESIRE).

And the wonderful account of Stephen. In the middle of his sermon before his stoning and heaven graduation, he quoted from Is. 66:1. "Heaven is my throne and earth is my footstool, where is the house you have built for me? Here O Lord have I prepared a resting place. Everyone before Jesus was under the law because they did not have the indwelling Holy Spirit. The river, and the fire in Stephen helped him through that last sermon. May I with great sensitivity say, though a young man, Stephen graduated to heaven. Don't take death on this earth so seriously, relocating to heaven is not a bad thing. We must take everyone there that we can.

Father, thank you for drawing me to Jesus. I repent of grieving you Holy Spirit, and I want the desire and hunger to pursue you. Thank you for baptizing me in the Holy Spirit. I receive Your fountain, Your river, and Your purging fire. In Christ name AMEN.

CHAPTER SIXTEEN
The Baptism of the Holy Spirit (Part 2)

Scripture Foundation

John 7:38 He who believes in Me, as the Scripture has said, out of his heart will flow rivers of living water.

Ephesian 2:22 In whom you also are being built together for a dwelling place of God in the Spirit.

SECRET: PRAYING IN THE HOLY SPIRIT- THE GREATEST UNVEILED SECRET IN CHRISTENDOM

We reach a place that is more important to me than you can imagine. Some will be tempted to remember spiritual wacko's and flakes, and again pass up your Acts 19 moment. Acts 1:8- Power will come when THE HOLY SPIRIT COMES ON YOU and in you. OH DO WE NEED POWER!

THE FAITH IN PURITY

Early Spring, I was 15 yrs old. My family had a few years of searching by the River of the Holy Spirit. Let's just say it wasn't too long, and we all fell in. I was up to mischief running around with interesting friends. I believe that day a game called snowball frenzy. We would hide behind bushes in front of houses, and hit cars with snowballs, then we would peel off in different directions after the thump. The gutsy moment came when it was a cop car. We never did get caught.

But I will never forget this incredible day. I jumped over the green fence at our house on 502 South St, walked in my house, and my folks, and brother were praying. So, I observed for a time before my Acts 19 moment came to visit. My brother Steve said, "would you like to receive the Holy Spirit." I said, "ok." As they laid hands on me.

My youthful fervor would take me into mischief, but I was so ready to yield to the Holy Spirit. I believe it was as simple as Jesus, baptize me in the Holy Spirit. I might describe it as warm honey pouring over me and hurts and fears seemed to vanish through tears that began deep inside and through my eyes. A dam began to break, and out of my adolescent being, born again spirit came a language from heaven. Organic would be a great way to describe a teen overwhelmed by the Spirit of God. Pride will not allow this damn to break. I simply accepted this gift, which I have learned in 40 years, is VERY difficult for some. Days later, I would sit down and write my first prophetic song, and yes from that time the scriptures came alive. I say prophetic songs because there are 2 clear things the Holy Spirit does. (Acts 19) He aids with a new prayer language, and prophecies into your life. I Still remember the scripture that became a song days later. Heb 13:15- Therefore by Him let us continually offer the sacrifice of praise to God, that is, the fruit of our lips, giving thanks to His name. THE FAITH IN PURITY is speaking Holy Spirit words, and faith rising from within your being, faith, and cleansing. I had a fountain in me from salvation (John 4) But that evening I was tapping into a river. John 7:39 (This He spoke of the Holy Spirit.) I was allowing the Holy Spirit to have my temple. 1000 times I've heard warnings from 1000 religious directions, be careful about this Holy Spirit stuff. Well I have a clear warning for all Generations. I Thessalonians 5:19-Do not quench the Holy Spirit.

I Corinthians 3:16, 17 Do you not know that you are the temple of God and that the Spirit of God dwells in you? If anyone defiles the temple of God, God will destroy him. For the temple of God is holy, which temple you are.

Be very picky how you lay your foundation. Your prayer life will increase 100 fold if you can pray to the Father in Jesus name with a Holy Spirit language. As I have said, pride will hinder this Acts 19 event faster than anything. Pride and the Holy Spirit cannot mix.

WAITING-As I've been writing this book, another topic rises at this moment. You say, I have asked for the Holy Spirit, and nothing happened. Well, when we arrive at the historic moment in Acts chapter 2, 50 days earlier there were 500 that were gathered. Please notice at the end of 50 days, only 120 were left. They were WAITING! Were you one that was left? Waiting is so difficult, being quiet is so difficult. Ask the troops behind Joshua for 7 days before the wall crashed down. Consider these amazing words in the bible: patience, longsuffering, endurance, self-control. Most of receiving the Holy Spirit is waiting for you to give up pride, and self so that He can become fountain, river, and fire. I am never so frustrated as when folks debate about 1 Corinthians 12, and 14, the antics of gifts, and tongues etc… How you dive into the Holy Spirit is your business. I am asking you to Get into your closet and ask Jesus to Fill You with the Holy Spirit. We must have power, and purity in these last days. You say, "I already have received." Then fast and pray and ask Him for a Daniel spirit, dreams, secrets and wisdom.

PRAYER- Jesus, you are my savior. Thank you for coming into me like a fountain, but I desire more. I ask you now to baptize me in the Holy Spirit, and as in Acts 19 may I pray in tongues and prophecy to the Glory of God. IN JESUS NAME AMEN.

CHAPTER SEVENTEEN
Proven Character

Scripture Foundation

Romans 5:3,4 Knowing that tribulation produces perseverance; perseverance, character; and character, hope.

Philippians 2:22 (Winning when no one is looking) But you know his proven character, that as a son with his father he served with me in the gospel.

SECRET: PSALMS 25:14-THE SECRET OF THE LORD IS WITH THEM THAT FEAR HIM

Let's spend some time with a character in the Old Testament. As Paul is like a father to Timothy, I'd like father David to speak to you about THE FAITH IN PURITY. In this chapter, our topic is proven character. This is about character, which comes after trials and perseverance.

WHAT DO YOU LOOK LIKE AFTER A FIERY

TRIAL AND AFTER YOU HAVE BEEN PUSHED TO THE LIMIT?

If a father could give a present to his son to build character, well, I guess the gems and council in Psalm 119 would be a prototype. Psalm 119 is the longest chapter in the Bible. There is not even a close second. This chapter results from my love for hidden gems in the Word.

David is believed to be the author of Psalm 119, written near the end of his life. Let me shock you with some numerical anomalies. Psalm 119 is arranged in an acrostic pattern. There are 22 letters in the Hebrew alphabet, and this psalm contains 22 units of 8 verses each. For your entertainment, I'd like to give you 22 Faith In Purity nuggets from this chapter as they relate to THE FAITH IN PURITY. When you are finished with this chapter, go back and read only the underlined phrases as an exercise.

Psalm 119

1. Vs 1 Blessed are the <u>undefiled in the way</u>, who walk in the law of the Lord!

2. Vs 9-11 How can a young man <u>cleanse his way</u>? By taking heed according to Your word. With my whole heart I have sought You; Oh, let me not wander from Your commandments! Your word I have hidden in my heart, that <u>I might not sin against You.</u>

3. Vs 18 <u>Open my eyes, that I may see</u> wondrous things from Your law.

4. Vs 25 My soul clings to the dust; <u>Revive me according to Your word.</u>

5. Vs 29 Remove from me the <u>way of lying</u> and grant me Your law graciously.

6. Vs 37 <u>Turn away my eyes from looking at worthless things,</u> and revive me in Your way.

7. Vs 38 Establish Your word to Your servant, who is <u>devoted to fearing You.</u>

8. Vs 48 I will lift up my hands to Your commandments, which I love and I will <u>meditate on Your statutes.</u>

9. Vs 59 I t<u>hought about my ways</u> and turned my feet to Your testimonies.

10. Vs 62 At <u>midnight I will rise to give thanks to You</u>, because of Your righteous judgments.

11. Vs 73 Your hands have made me and fashioned me; <u>give me understanding</u>, that I may learn Your commandments.

12. Vs 101 I have <u>restrained my feet from every evil way</u>, that I may keep Your word.

13. Vs 105 Your word is a <u>lamp to my feet and a light to my path.</u>

14. Vs 114 <u>You are my hiding place and my shield</u>; I hope in Your word.

15. Vs 116 <u>Uphold me according to Your word</u>, that I may live; and <u>do not let me be ashamed of my hope.</u>

16. Vs 125 I am Your servant; <u>give me understanding</u>, that I may know Your testimonies

17. Vs 130 <u>The entrance of Your words gives light; it gives understanding to the simple</u> (naive).

18. Vs 133 Direct my steps by Your word, and <u>let no iniquity have dominion over me.</u>

19. Vs 140 <u>Your word is very pure</u>; therefore your servant loves it.

20. Vs 148 My eyes are awake through the night watches, that <u>I may meditate on Your word</u>.

21. Vs 165 Great peace have those who love Your law, and <u>nothing causes them to stumble</u>. (KJV- Nothing shall offend them)

22. Vs 172 <u>My tongue shall speak of Your word</u>, for all Your commandments are righteousness.

Psalm 119 wants to establish in us THE FAITH IN PURITY. While we are in Psalms, chapter 19 also contains some magnificent truths about purity. Let's blast our soul with 22 PURITY nuggets from the beautiful Psalm 19.

7 The law of the Lord is perfect, <u>converting the soul;</u>

The testimony of the Lord is sure, <u>making wise the simple (naive);</u>

THE FAITH IN PURITY

8 The statutes of the Lord are right, <u>rejoicing the heart;The commandment of the Lord is pure, / enlightening the eyes;</u>

9 The fear of the Lord is <u>clean, enduring forever;</u> The judgments of the Lord are true and righteous altogether.

10 More to be <u>desired are they than gold</u>, Yea, than much fine <u>gold; (refined)</u> Sweeter also than <u>honey and the honeycomb.</u>

11 Moreover <u>by them Your servant is warned,</u> And in <u>keeping them there is great reward. Who can understand his errors? Cleanse me from secret faults.</u> Keep back Your servant also <u>from presumptuous sins; Let them not have dominion over me.</u> Then I shall be blameless, And I shall <u>be innocent of great transgression.</u> Let the <u>words of my mouth and/ the meditation of my heart Be acceptable in Your sight, O Lord, my strength and my Redeemer.</u>

So there's 44 nuggets from two amazing chapters in the bible. It truly is amazing how many things point us toward renewing the mind, and meditation, and purity.

Holy Spirit, let the words of my mouth and the meditation of my heart be acceptable to you. Lord let me write my own psalms, and my own code of moral conduct. Use my creativity to set me on a strong course of purity. In Christ name, AMEN

CHAPTER EIGHTEEN
Put On Him, Put Off ME

Scripture Foundation

Ephesians 6:11 Put on the whole armor of God, that you may be able to stand against the wiles of the devil.

Colossians 2:20-23 (NKJV) Therefore, if you died with Christ from the basic principles of the world, why, as though living in the world, do you subject yourselves to regulations 21 "Do not touch, do not taste, do not handle," 22 which all concern things which perish with the using—according to the commandments and doctrines of men? 23 These things indeed have an appearance of wisdom in self-imposed religion, false humility, and neglect of the body, but are of no value against the indulgence of the flesh.

SECRET: YOUR ARMOR DOES NOT COVER YOUR BACKSIDE, ALWAYS FACE YOUR

ENEMY

For sure those three verses belong together. RESTRAINING SENSUAL INDULGENCES, AMEN! I will paraphrase earlier verses in 22 items in this chapter to bring context.

1 Be rooted in Christ, seek things above 2 be built on Him. 3 Set your mind on things above. 4 Your faith will grow strong in the truth. 5 Growing in truth will result in thankfulness. 6 Don't grab empty philosophies from human thinking, 7 Only think of Christ. 8 You were baptized with Christ 9 Raised from the dead with Christ. 10. Your life is hidden with God in Christ, He forgave your sins, 11 put to death fornication, uncleanness, lust, evil desire, idolatry 12 Put off anger, wrath, malice, blasphemy, swearing, 13 Put on a new man in knowledge after the image of your Creator 14 put on tender mercies, meekness, kindness, humility, long suffering 15 bearing one another and forgiving one another 16 He canceled all records and 17 nailed them to the cross. 18 He took the devil, and publicly shamed him. 19 There is no condemnation in how you eat and drink or worship. 20 I am buried with Christ (dying to self) 21 raising up with Him (take your authority with Him in the heavenly) 22 If Christ has not motivated the way I live, it will not help fight off evil desire.

We live in quite a culture that is satisfied, yet

anemic, deaf, and hurting. When I visited Africa, they worshiped for an hour, and they were just getting started. A service can go three hours, and they devour every minute. They have no TV, nice homes, or refrigerators. They have a hut the size of your kitchen for a family of 8-10. Yet, they have great faith because they are not distracted by hypocrisy and good works. We must put on a HUNGER.

In my life, I will never forget watching a packed church in India. 100% of them with their hands in the air, eyes screwed shut, screaming and loving on Master Jesus for 40-45 minutes straight, with no care of what others thought except Jesus. They have no other option but desperation and to throw themselves at the mercy of Father God. It's possible in some of those areas, they might walk out of the church and be abandoned by their family because of Jesus. Oh, the faith that was in that room. We must put on THANKFULNESS.

Much of Colossians 2 and 3 are instructions related to dying to the flesh, putting off the flesh, and putting on things of the Spirit. This may sound a little foreign to you, and I understand that. Our life as a follower of Jesus is a progression in maturity. My life changed at a crucial moment when I was eighteen. I realized most of my relationships only had hay and stubble as a foundation. I lived at a surface-level and often was not honoring God. I knelt before the cross and repented, and I knew I needed to do two things. I worked in a job with noise, and most of the time, it was routine repetitive work. First, I wrote scriptures by hand on a piece of paper. Scriptures such as Romans 8:1, 6:21,23, Ephesians 6:10-19, Mark 11;23,24, John 3:16, John 8:31,32, John 10:10, John 14:1-4 & 26, 16:13, 2 Corinthians 10:4,5 and the book of Romans 12. I would pull them out of my pocket and memorize them. Most of them I still know today. The second thing I knew to do was to pray in the Spirit. Put on the WORD and PRAYER.

It seemed the devil himself would stand before me at times and assault me with thoughts and imaginations. "You're a loser Pomp!" So, with no exaggeration, at times, I prayed in the Holy Spirit for three, four, five or more hours. Jude 20

I was always in a battle, but, oh, the blessing. As I look back, I was burning off chaff and putting on Colossians 3:12-14, which is: tender mercies, kindness, humility, meekness, long suffering; bearing with one another, and forgiving one another, if anyone has a complaint against another; even as Christ forgave you, so you also must do. But above all, these things put on love, which is the bond of perfection. And let the peace of God rule in your hearts.

Your destiny will be one of two things, what you put on, or what you put off. Stand and face your enemy with full armor on, and pray always with all prayer and supplication. EPHESIANS 6:18a—PRAYING ALWAYS WITH ALL PRAYER AND SUPPLICATION IN THE SPIRIT

Sweet Holy Spirit, the laws of man and my striving will not resolve the works of my flesh. Let me keep a pattern of putting me off and putting You on. I am hidden in Christ. I am buried with you, and I am raised up with you. In Christ name, AMEN

CHAPTER NINETEEN
Pursue A Pure Heart

Scripture Foundation

1 Thesselonians 4:4,5a-that each of you should know how to possess his own vessel in sanctification and honor, not in passion of lust

2 Timothy 2:22 (Winning the battle of lust) Flee also youthful lusts; but pursue righteousness, faith, love, peace with those who call on the Lord out of a pure heart.

SECRET: EXAGGERATION COULD SAVE YOUR LIFE

So we reached this milestone when the clock struck 2:22. 2 Tim 2:22 was the first thing that popped into my mind. Here is my interpretation of this verse. Keep the faith in purity through the laborious process of fleeing tangible impulses. The result will be righteousness, faith, love and peace as long as purity is present. Rom 14:17- The kingdom of God is not eat nor drink, but righteousness, peace and joy in the Holy Ghost.

So, I am asking Jesus to give you BOLDNESS like THE LION to pursue the right things. Remember Joseph violently fleeing Pharaoh's Wife as she was likely exposing herself to him. This picture represents the point: do not throw away your confidence in an instant. Heb 10:35. if we hold fast the confidence and the rejoicing of the hope firm to the end. Heb 3:6b. Assault on your purity shows up on billboards, and phones, and iPad, and even the way many folks dress. WHEN IT COMES YOUR WAY, YOU MUST FLEE. But character is when no one is looking. Joseph so believed in the dream from God, an impulse and temptation could not steal HIS FAITH. Yes, there were years of jail time to develop his faith and prophetic skills. But his dream stayed strong with his confidence.

Keep faith through the laborious process of fleeing new and old tangible impulses. Many battles would define the time for me between 18, and 22 when I got married, yes 22. The story will come later, but a Goliath figure tried to destroy me at 14. 4-5 years later I became very active socially, with guys and girls. Honestly my wife was the only gal that I really fell in love with. I had a time in Florida, when I was pursuing Cathy, my wife to be. I had priceless skills of memorizing the Word, and praying in the Spirit, and a culture of worship. My first ministry spot was in south Florida. Let's just say that girls didn't wear much in the public. Again, I set my face hard to stay pure. I had a personal exaggerated Covenant that if I were to look upon a woman wrongfully, that divorce would be in my future. Job 31:1-I have made a covenant with my eyes; why then should I look upon a young woman?

This time in South Florida represented my ideal prototype for pursuing the right things. The Word, and a wonderful person named Cathy! I memorized more scripture, and I Prayed in the Spirit, and in English with passion. After 38 years of marriage, with honesty and before my wife, I had my valleys of lust and wrong passion. Single guys and gals, you must exaggerate the WORD OF GOD STANDARDS IN PURITY, you will not regret it. Wives, don't allow your husband to be idle, and wander. Men, cover your wives, take authority in your home, pray, and let the WORD be the center. Blow up scriptures and plaster it on the walls! If you love each other, that glorious spirit-to-spirit will happen. You must make it happen. ONCE AGAIN YOUR CHOICE! Yes, we both had issues, the hardest times were when condemnation would cause us to judge instead of giving grace in situations.

THE GREAT PURSUIT-2 Tim 2:22-Follow with boldness after righteousness. If you have not memorized 2 Cor. 5:21 now is the time: For He was made to be sin for us who knew no sin that we might be made the righteousness of God in Christ. Boldly run after Faith- 2 Cor 5:7-For we walk by Faith, not by sight. Col 3:14- But above all things put on Love which is the bond of perfection, and boldly pursue Peace- Ps 34:14-Depart from evil, and do good, seek peace and pursue it. Rom 14:19- pursue things which make for peace, and things by which one may edify another—Heb 12:14-pursue Peace with all people, and holiness, without which no one will see the Lord.

Father, In Jesus name I commit to run after righteousness, and faith and purity. I take a stand in the strongholds of my life. I will memorize your Word, I will pray in the Holy Spirit. I will hold firm on my chest the breastplate of righteousness. In Christ Name AMEN

The Lion, By Tim Pomp

So as in nature one animal RULER, yes the King of the Jungle

As others bow down and cower, and before him act humble

A Lion shows strength and boldness, a voice loud and clear

Every eye watches, shutters, and trembles in utter fear

So it happened one sad day when Satan fell in pride

His motives, his shame, his fear behind it he did hide

He started the battle that until the lake of fire he will be

Roaring like a lion but he's toothless, and has no creativity

Until that judgment day when the battle is finally over

You and I must stand my friend, courage it must cover

Not the courage devised with grit, the grit of self-made- man

But from the Lion of the tribe of Judah, In His life you'll stand

So seven things will prove to be where confidence is shown

Seven things will Prove--- Christ is the Victor's Crown

First applying Jesus precious blood, just one drop will do

Through His hands and feet & side, He bled for me and you

Then the veil was torn in two, yes the law, endless sacrifice

Our veil was lifted, and shame is gone, fear no more a vice

So grace exploded, door was opened a new time of grace

Faith would be the pleasing song, and boldness on the face

Love then screamed, forgiveness too, yes the Agape kind

Boldness comes, in the day of judgment, spirit, soul, mind

Salvation by grace & through faith, one more thing to do

Be Baptized in the Holy Ghost and boldness will come on you

Ephesians 6 gives the next, put on the full armor of God

Utterance given, boldness with words everywhere you trod

Alas the King, the clincher, the Light, the Truth, the liberator

It Is Quick, and powerful, sharp, and shatters like, a hammer

Yes the Word of God that stands forever,

It roars with affirmation to the believer

That fear and shame have no more power

I walk with boldness like a Lion until the final hour

Heb 10:35,38 "Therefore do not cast away your confidence, which has great reward. Now the just shall live by faith; But if anyone draws back, My soul has no pleasure in him."

CHAPTER TWENTY
The Sufferings Of Christ

SCRIPTURE FOUNDATION

2 TIMOTHY 3:12 YES, AND ALL WHO DESIRE TO LIVE GODLY IN CHRIST JESUS WILL SUFFER PERSECUTION.

1 PETER 2:21-23 FOR TO THIS YOU WERE CALLED, BECAUSE CHRIST ALSO SUFFERED FOR US, LEAVING US AN EXAMPLE, THAT YOU SHOULD FOLLOW HIS STEPS: "WHO COMMITTED NO SIN, NOR WAS DECEIT FOUND IN HIS MOUTH"; WHO, WHEN HE WAS REVILED, DID NOT REVILE IN RETURN; WHEN HE SUFFERED, HE DID NOT THREATEN, BUT COMMITTED HIMSELF TO HIM WHO JUDGES RIGHTEOUSLY.

SECRET: WOUNDEDNESS IS A GIFT

We arrive at a subject that is not popular. I hope you're ready to again find the gem of purity through looking at the tragedy of the cross. Surrounded on both sides of 1 Pet 2 verse 22 is suffering. 1. Christ suffered for us as our example. 2.

Christ suffered for us and left the judgment to His Father.

Let's be honest, there's really nothing fun in this chapter. It begins with Jesus the stone of stumbling, the rock offense. Matt. 21:44-We have one of 2 choices: we can fall on the rock and be broken, or it will fall on us and be powder. Ps 51:17-The sacrifices of God are a broken spirit, a broken and a contrite heart—these, O God, You will not despise. Then there is submission to the government, to your master, and to your spouse. The fun continues: keep your tongue from deceit and evil, and you will suffer for right and wrong. Thank you very much Peter!

But WAIT: look at 1 Peter 2:24. He bore our sins in His body on the tree, so that we could die to sin and live to righteousness, and by His stripes we were healed. Purity and righteousness come because of His suffering. He heals my trauma, and wounds because I embrace His stripes. We can, but we don't have to die to sin. We can, but we don't have to be pure, and have strong faith.

(Phil 3:10) "That I may know Him and the power of His resurrection and the fellowship of His sufferings, being conformed to His death". The issue of purity begins with the relationship to Christ, KNOWING HIM. Why did Paul have to stick suffering in there? Again a story to come I

THE FAITH IN PURITY

have no idea how the Holy Spirit showed up in my room and supernaturally showed me how to forgive someone who just assaulted me. (Mom's and dad's prayers would be my guess) But I will never forget the multiple freedoms that came when that umbilical cord was cut. Anger and murder just fell to the floor. The pain of my suffering related to Jesus on the cross. Forgiveness was the result. Of course, my pain did not compare to His.

What does that mean, the fellowship of his sufferings? It means I do the same thing He did when He was bruised and beaten. Judgment is always the Father's business.

The other topic, putting the members of my flesh to death so that Jesus can make me pure and righteous. Then faith can rise in me and please Father.

Matt 16:24-Then Jesus said to His disciples, "If anyone desires to come after Me, let him deny himself, and take up his cross, and follow Me. I must often remember, and go to the cross, (bread and wine) but He has not called me to stay there. That I may know Him and the Power of His resurrection. Purity, and faith will be in the power of His resurrection. What does God look like? Like one with the heart to give up His son, His only Son. One that would allow Him to suffer beyond comprehension for you and me. (Heb 1:3). He is the "express image" of God. But the resurrection shows us that HE IS ALWAYS VICTORIOUS. The enemy is defeated. He has crushed Satan under His feet. Hallelujah. Woundedness is a gift if you see it as a gift. If you are always a victim, well, then you will always need sympathy. One who is wounded, and goes to the cross and the empty tomb will see their wounds as a GIFT! Redemption will be the SONG OF YOUR HEART because of His suffering. I am victorious, but I do know Him and the fellowship of His Sufferings.

Father, I want mercy and grace in my suffering. I am not a victim, I am an overcomer. I am entitled to embrace your death and resurrection. Lord, let Faith and Purity come from my hurts and wounds. In Christ name AMEN

CHAPTER TWENTY ONE
What If

Scriptural Foundation

2 Samuel 11:1b But David remained at Jerusalem.

Acts 16:6b-they were forbidden by the Holy Spirit to preach the word in Asia.

2 Peter 2:21,22 Winning over religious spirit and stupidity) "It would have been better for them not to have known the way of righteousness, than to have known it and then to turn their backs on the sacred command that was passed on to them. Of them the proverbs are true: "A dog returns to its vomit," and, "A sow that is washed returns to her wallowing in the mud."

SECRET: THERE'S NO "IF" IN "YES HOLY SPIRIT"

Here's an overview of 2 Peter chapter 2. God is good all the time. God hates the spirit behind Pharisee, and false teachers who twist the scriptures to fit their lifestyle. Get unbelief OUT or you won't have faith! Earlier in 2 Pet chapter 2 he begins with the "IF" IF God did not spare the angels who rebelled in heaven but sent them to hell forever. IF God did not spare the ancient world, but judgment came through water, grace was found by Noah+7. God knows how to deliver the godly out of temptation.

So here we are in the 2000's. IF the Lord comes back soon, He is simply asking for a pure bride, and nothing unholy will enter His kingdom. 2 Peter 2:9 says "if this is so, then the Lord knows how to rescue the godly from trials and to hold the unrighteous for punishment on the day of judgment." God is good, but judgment is inevitable. Judgment is the punishment of sin. And for the believer, affirmation of FAITHFULNESS AND RIGHTEOUSNESS IN CHRIST. Faith and Grace can only stop the Judgment of sin. Yes, by Grace you are saved through faith. GET SIN OUT, AND DON'T TEACH YOURSELF AND OTHERS BY TWISTING THE SCRIPTURE TO FIT YOUR LIFE.

But David remained in Jerusalem, 2 Samuel 11:1, what does this mean? Yes, David stayed home, and the entire debacle of Bathsheba unfolded. In life, there are UP TIMES AND DOWN TIMES. Remember character is exposed when no one is looking. Follow the words, depression, defraud, deceit, defile, victim and you will find an alone place with nobody checking on you. A place when you have won, or lost a great battle. A place when you deserve to be alone with a bad movie, a bag of chips and a giant chocolate shake. Inevitably, you will run into Bathsheba, leading yourself to a place where you cannot righteously fulfill your desires. (DEFRAUD)

What if David would have gone to war? This debacle and a dead baby and murder would not have happened. What if the Lord would have FORBIDDEN David to stay home? Well He probably did, but he wasn't listening. But Father can always bring redemption. Look at Psalm 51 and you get forgiveness to a rascal who did not deserve it. There you will find humility, brokenness, remorse, and crying for the Holy Spirit not to leave. He did not leave, and David still was the man after God's own heart.

1 Timothy 2:15 - Be diligent to present yourself approved to God, a worker who does not need to be ashamed, rightly dividing the word of truth. Having your SWORD, and rightly dividing will take out the WHAT IF'S. When you are working in his will, shame will not be an issue. The issue, dividing the word of truth.

David got sick of eating a buffet in a pig pin. Notice 2 Peter 2:22, "A sow that is washed returns to her wallowing in the mud." A sow that is washed: Interesting. A pig taking a shower? Yes, thank the Lord that we can be forgiven. Thank you, Lord, for the cleansing bath of the blood of Jesus.

Prayer—Jesus, it is the end times. Forgive me for any false teaching that I hold on to. I reject any motives in me that are connected to a religious spirit. I hate pretty on the outside, and ugly and vile on the inside. I will go and work, and fight. In victories, and down times I will stay protected by your WORD. May it not be said of me, WHAT IF! I submit myself to a church or a mentor to purge out the stubborn religious spirit. In Jesus Name AMEN

CHAPTER TWENTY TWO
The Faith In Purity

Scripture Foundation

James 2:22-(Winning over Doubt) Do you see that faith was working together with his works, and by works faith was made perfect?

James 2:3-and you pay attention to the one wearing the fine clothes and say to him, "You sit here in a good place

SECRET: FAITH IN PURITY TEST—HONOR

Here's the paraphrase of this epic Faith in Purity James 2 -Be extremely careful how you treat one person over another. It will ruin your faith if you are prejudiced. In fact, if you claim the name of Jesus, and I'll-treat another, it is the same as blaspheming. Keep on with impure motives toward others, and the end result will be judgment without mercy. You are a liar if you say you have faith and sit on your bottom and proclaim yourself as good. Faith without works is dead. Do you have pure hope, which is the make-up of faith, then get up and do something, and faith will explode for you. Do you want me to be impressed that you believe? The devils also believe! Consider Abraham and Isaac, take everything to mount Moriah, and your covenant of faith begins. Then verse 22- Do you see that faith was working together with his works, and by works faith was made perfect?

WHAT A MONTAGE REGARDING THE FAITH IN PURITY!

Abraham believed, and as he believed in God, IT BECAME RIGHTEOUSNESS. How does one know that he is righteous? It is when you are tested to the max. Your pure response resolves the equation; Trials plus your absolute belief in Father will equal RIGHTEOUSNESS. Doubt, unbelief, and impurity will result in sin.

Once again with detail we begin to define THE FAITH IN PURITY. What is behind what you DO for Jesus? What are your motives behind your dealings with people?

Years ago, I was tested with an evangelist that has a worldwide ministry. A man and his wife that have seen many thousands saved, healed and delivered. Impeccable character, and upright people. I seemed to be in the circle of this person a few times a year, and in short, I didn't like this person at all. 100%

my stuff, and each year it seemed he would show up where I was:) And each time I wanted to put a tack on his chair or something like that. Make it clear, this man had never done anything to me, this evil was purely mine. (I was kind of smelling like pigs) So, Holy Spirit dealt with me very strongly, and sure enough there he was in another meeting I was in, sitting on the front row. Faith without works is dead? There was a break in the service, and I leaned to my honey and said, write a check for $$$$ to this ministry. I walked up to this man, handed the check, knelt, grabbed his hand, prayed, and blessed his ministry with tears in my eyes. He had no idea what was happening, and I didn't tell him. The ill feelings vanished and are gone forever.

So, to continue this incredible thought, as we go with His desire foremost in our thoughts, His faith becomes perfected. In James it says of patience, let it work, and you will be perfect and lacking nothing. In 2 Peter 1:4-8, there is a mountain of virtues that end in the bond of perfection, love. Walk them out and verse 10 says you will never stumble. Your faith can be made perfect if you KEEP GOING! Patience is such a great description of the PAIN and affliction of faith. But faith is what pleases God!

Father, in Jesus' name, and by the Holy Spokesperson; Holy Spirit, let me be a doer, and not just a hearer. Let me show my pure hope by getting up and doing, and it will explode into FAITH. I begin in my life the CULTURE OF THE FAITH IN PURITY, In Christ Name AMEN!

CHAPTER TWENTY THREE
HE THAT OVERCOMETH

SCRIPTURE FOUNDATION

REVELATION 2:22 BEHOLD, I WILL CAST HER INTO A BED, AND THOSE THAT COMMIT ADULTERY WITH HER INTO GREAT TRIBULATION, EXCEPT THEY REPENT OF THEIR DEEDS.

MATTHEW 5:28 WHOEVER LOOKS AT A WOMAN TO LUST FOR HER HAS ALREADY COMMITTED ADULTERY WITH HER IN HIS HEART.

SECRET: HE'S GIVEN YOU A HIDDEN NAME

How about a paraphrase of 22 items out of Revelations 2.

Nevertheless, I have this against you, you have left your first love. 2 Remember therefore from whence thou art fallen, and repent, and do the first works; 3. or else I will come unto thee quickly, and will remove your candlestick out of his place, except you repent. 4. He that hath an ear, let him hear. 5 To him that overcomes will I give to eat of the tree of life. 6 The devil shall cast some of you into prison, that you may be tried. 7 be thou faithful unto death, and I will give a crown of life. 8 He that overcomes shall not be hurt of the second death. 9 Repent; or else I will come unto thee quickly, 10 I will fight against them with the sword of my mouth. 11 To him that overcomes will I give to eat of the hidden manna. 12 I will give him a white stone, and in the stone a new name written. 13 No man knows it save he that receiveth it. 14 These things saith the Son of God 15 who hath his eyes like unto a flame of fire. 16 and his feet are like fine brass; 17 I know thy works, and charity, 18 and service, and faith, 19 and patience, and works.20-And I gave her space to repent of her fornication; and she repented not. 21-Behold, I will cast her into a bed, and those who commit adultery with her into great tribulation. 22 Except they repent of their deeds.

Another 2:22 coincidence, repent of adultery? The unveiling, (apocalyptic) outpouring is happening. I would like to highlight the topic of my next book. BOOK 2 THE FAITH IN PURITY, PUTTING CHRIST FIRST. As mentioned above, have you lost your first love? What would it be like if you nurtured that first water and fire when you were born again. The answer; the fountain would be a river, and the fire would be gold, silver and precious stones refining in you. It's your choice, baby, teen, son, or mature.

Let's say it plain, who are you in bed with, HOPE OR DELILAH? (See Judges chapters 13-16) There is no greater example to me than to look at my marriage with the one who I know better than anyone on this earth. Because I know my beloved, it is very difficult to play the pretense game. Because I know her and exchange HOPE with her every day. We cannot lead ourselves to a place where we cannot righteously fulfill our desires. (defraud) The reason, spirit-to-spirit fellowship. Oh I love that ! The moment I put on the mask, and hide motives; irritation, anger and shame rise and all is not well. My authority immediately weakens and flesh rises! But that spirit covenant MUST CONTINUE. This entire book is about this principle, to know Him and the power of His resurrection. To have motives that are PURE, to allow great FAITH.

So, let's conclude with 3 powerful descriptions of the heart of this chapter, OVERCOMING FAITH.

1. <u>To him that overcomes will I give to eat of the tree of life.</u> In context to growing, eating would be quite significant. If you eat His flesh, and drink His blood, you will live. Revelations 22:2

John 6:66, no kidding, the moment Jesus asked disciples to eat His flesh and drink blood, they turned from Him. The tree of life which bears twelve kinds of fruits, and yields her fruit every month. Don't tell me this is boring, uncovering these things from the tree of life WILL CHANGE YOUR LIFE, OFTEN.

2. <u>He who overcomes will not be hurt by the second death.</u> Our 2:22 passage is talking about adultery in the setting of the end times. Who you are in bed with is not necessarily a person. It could be anger, laziness, fear, hurt, food, religion, pride, shame, victim mentality. But those things are not my fault! It will never matter. If your life is hidden with Christ in God, you will not be hurt, or afraid of the second death.

3. <u>To him that overcomes I will give hidden manna, and will give him a white stone, and in the stone a new name written, which no man knoweth saving he that receiveth it.</u> There's that "hidden" word. I'm telling you, you were made to uncover secrets, don't give up, keep searching. One time I was asking the Father, who am I? Lord am I a pastor, a prophet, a teacher, a worship leader? He answered me so clearly in my heart and it has never left me. He said to me, "Timothy, you are a

minister of Hope." My friends, I don't care what anyone else calls me, I will never forget that title that He gave to me. Please ask Him what your secret name is. Our FAITH IN PURITY GOAL- BE AN OVERCOMER!

Father, in Jesus name I pray that my friend would find The Faith that comes from a pure life. I'm a conqueror, I'm victorious, I'm reigning with Jesus. May the Holy Spirit lead them to search for their name, their mission, their treasure that is found in the uncompromised Word of God. May PURE HOPE become THE FAITH IN PURITY. AMEN

CHAPTER TWENTY FOUR
The Number 22

Scripture Foundation

Daniel 5:12-Inasmuch as an excellent spirit, knowledge, understanding, interpreting dreams, solving riddles, and explaining enigmas were found in this Daniel.

SECRET: PSALMS 22-JESUS ON THE CROSS

Make it very clear, I am not magnifying a magic number! You can google new age, and find cosmic creations from numbers. It's not about a number, this is about a father sharing divine secrets to his creation. When I see the numbers 22, or 2:22, or 2222, I simply get quickened about staying pure. When I see 333, it's something different, and 3:16, and 4:12, and 23, and 40 etc. His Word explodes in me many times in conjunction with a number. I NEED HELP! When God gives you something, His creativity and the Holy Spirit will teach you all things John 14:26b. 22 is simply my secret code for the confusion, and duplicity of LUST, and wrong motives.

What is the reason for spiritual immaturity? Believers don't expose, and destroy confusion. The Word in you should be able to divide good and evil, joints and marrow, soul and spirit. Hebrews 4:12. The number 22, which is double eleven (which symbolizes disorder and chaos), can represent a concentration of disorganization. Jeroboam I, the very first king of Israel after the United Kingdom split in two in 930 B.C., reigned for 22 years (930 to 909 B.C.). Ahab, considered the WORST Israelite king, also reigned for 22 years (874 to 853 B.C.). King Amon, who ruled for only two years and is consider one of the worst kings over Judah, began his rule at the age of twenty-two

The Hebrew alphabet is made up of 22 letters, which are used to compose the Word of God. The word of God is called a lamp (Psalms 119:105, Proverbs 6:22), thus it is the light by which we are to live. The word light is found 264 times in Scripture. When 264 is divided by 12 (divine authority) we have 22, which represents light. God created twenty-two things in the six days of creation.

There are twenty-two books in the Aaronic (Levitical) Old Testament, which is the light of

God for Israel. There are twenty-two generations from Adam to Jacob. When Moses raised up the tabernacle of God there were exactly 22,000 Levites consecrated to serve.

The word light is used twenty-two times in the Gospel of John. The 22nd time John uses the word, he quotes Jesus: "I have come as a light into the world." (John 12:46). Christians are to walk in the light of Christ (John 3:21) and be the light of the world (Matthew 5:14 -15).

The apostle Paul's epistle to the Hebrews, written to Greek-speaking Jews and Gentiles, is the 22nd book of the New Testament.

And the key of the house of David will I lay upon his shoulder; so he shall open, and none shall shut; and he shall shut, and none shall open. -Isaiah 22.22

The Number 22 can be the Number of Revelation. It governs the overall structure of Scripture, from the 22 Spokes of the Bible Wheel to the Twenty-two Spokes of the Inner Wheel of Revelation. Currently in political prophetic revelation, the number 22 is huge.

Teach me thy way, O LORD; I will walk in thy truth: unite my heart to fear thy name. Psalm 86.1

The Number 22 unites the entire body of Scripture - The phrase "unite my heart" is numerically equivalent to the Hebrew word for the

Wheel. My take, a wheel describes an object that is perfectly succinct, and round, and powerfully UNITED as the spokes all work together.

The Number 22 unites the entire Bible in the form of the Wheel, and the Wheel (Galgal = 66) unites the heart of all 66 Books of the Holy Bible, and all of this is united in the complicated structure of the Greek and Hebrew languages! Three Cycles of 22 Books united in One perfect Circle. Three in one. Divine perfection bursting forth! Thank you, Father, Son and Holy Spirit! Yes, anyone can find those facts by research. If you can't wrap your head around it all, neither can I, but it would have been hard to leave out those facts.

Let's take a moment in the wonderment of Psalms 22. If ever you needed pure hope regarding the validity and authenticity of scripture, just go to the old testament and learn about Jesus. The secret of exactly how many prophecies Jesus fulfilled right down to His birth, words on the cross, beatings, and humility etc. are probably more than 400. Take a marker this year and find some for yourself.

Imagine David sitting in God's presence doing his thing, praising, writing, and these strange things come to him that I'm guessing he didn't even understand. What would make a man sit there and write words such as, "they pierced my hands and feet." Answer, the Prophetic Holy Spirit. Trust me, Buddhists and Muslims don't have a RISEN KING and they don't have hundreds of direct prophecies, as we do, that point straight to Jesus.   I'll give you 22 of these prophecies from Psalms 22 just regarding the CROSS. 1 My God, My God, why hast thou forsaken me 2. You are Holy enthroned on the praises of Israel 3. They cried to You and you were delivered 4. They cried to you and were not ashamed 5. I am a worm; a reproach to man, and despised by all. 6. All those who see me ridicule me. 7. I am poured out like water. 8. All my bones are out of joint 9. My heart is like wax, it has melted within Me 10. My strength has dried up 11. My tongue clings to my jaws 12. You have laid me in the dust of death 13. For dogs have surrounded me. 14. The congregation of the wicked have enclosed me 15. They pierced my hands and my feet 16. I can count all my bones 17. They look at me and stare 18. They divide my garments among them. 19. And for my clothes they cast lots. 20 Yahweh, please don't stay far away. 21. Save me from this violent death, from these dogs. 22. Save me from the power of the enemy, from the roaring lion.

  May I take a bit of liberty with the AMEN, the final words of the bible. IT WOULD BE REVELATIONS 22:22, though there are only 21 verses. Yes, I understand the warning of adding to the scriptures, I'm just adding a 22 AMEN!

Revelations 22:20-YES,I AM COMING SOON

Revelations 22:21-MAY THE GRACE OF THE LORD BE WITH GOD'S HOLY PEOPLE

VS 22-AMEN-FOR EVER AND EVER AND EVER AND EVER!

Father, I am astounded by the Word of God. I ask you to give me keys to unlock treasure from your word. I open the door of my heart to receive your truth. May I find Jesus as I read the Old Testament. May the Word be a lamp to my feet and a light to my path. I repent and turn from all confusion, and darkness. In Christ name, AMEN.

THE FAITH IN PURITY

CHAPTER TWENTY FIVE
Prophesying Over My Potential

Scripture Foundation

Jeremiah 1:10b- to root out, to pull down, to destroy, to throw down, to build and to plant.

Jeremiah 29:13-And you will seek Me and find Me, when you search for Me with all your heart.

SECRET: MY QUALIFICATION-YOUNG, OLD, SON, DAUGHTER

It is the Glory of God to Conceal a matter, but it is the Glory of a king to search out a matter. Proverbs 25:2. I love puzzles and word definitions, and mysteries, cracking secret's, it is built in my DNA. No, I'm not always so good at it. I do believe there is a secret in Joel 2:28,29 when he said, "your sons and daughters will prophesy, your old men will dream dreams, and young men will see visions." In each of those Holy Spirit gifts include the interpretation of, and the discovery of, and the unveiling of! These elements are missing from the church today. I am asking you to lean in and ask Father to fuel your imagination and set you on a new venture of creativity. Let's reflect again, one of the greatest examples of purity in the bible has to be Daniel. In short, he fasted pleasantries, he prayed 3 times a day un-ashamedly, and he saw things like no one else saw. How do you know that you are maturing in Christ? According to Jeremiah, when you learn how to root out, pull down and destroy, then you build and plant. Daniel seemed to master all of these things, and he changed a nation through his faith and purity.

In Jesus' name may GENERATIONAL SHAME AND FEAR TO BE BROKEN. May Jesus BREAK YOU OUT OF SLUMBER, AND LAZY. I DESIRE TO PUSH YOU INTO DREAMS, VISIONS, AND PROPHECY, of course from the Holy Spirit. Miles Monroe said, "the wealthiest place in the world is not the gold, or diamond mines of South Africa, or the oil fields of Iran. The wealthiest place in the world is the cemetery. In it lie books never written, masterpieces never painted, inventions that we never made".

What percentage of those dreams six feet under were squelched because of idols and wrong motives? Without purity, faith will not come, thus your dreams and visions and full potential will not be fulfilled. So our goal is to root out, and destroy those strongholds. After that with His prophecies, dreams and visions, we build and plant.

The moral compass of our world is messed up! As in 1 Sam. 3:1- the Word or the Lord, and the constant hearing of his voice is rare today"! The sanctity of marriage, the honor of children to parents is greatly challenged in our lifetime. And maybe the biggest 21st century curse of all is the Facebook, texting, google age that again is making us void of true communication. Yes, I use Facebook, and all the above, but Lord help us use them properly. Father help us begin to uproot things not from you, and begin planting and building upon your WORD. I am asking you that if you have been taught that dreams, vision, and prophecy is just for a select few, understand that is a lie. Your criteria is that you are young, and old, sons and daughters. Excuses are usually related to, I am too lazy to die to me, and live to His creative workings. IT IS ABOUT EMPHATICALLY SEEKING HIM, AND YOU WILL FIND HIM!

1 Corinthians 14:1- Desire the best gifts, but especially that you may prophecy. Let's not make this any more complicated than it is. You will be prophesying either life or death over your destiny. Which one have you chosen? I am asking you to let the Holy Spirit dominate and dictate your desires and passion. Let's let a timeless scripture explode in you right now- Psalms 37:4-6 Delight yourself

also in the Lord, and HE WILL GIVE YOU THE DESIRES of your heart. Commit your way to the Lord, trust also in Him, and He shall bring it to pass. He shall bring forth your righteousness as the light, and your justice as the noonday.

Holy Spirit, I put my life before you and ask that from this day YOU will be my destiny. I will not be motivated to waste my life without fulfilling my potential. I am your son, daughter, young, or old, I ask you to give me dreams, visions, and prophetic words, to build your kingdom. I aggressively pursue life today. I ask you to unfold the secret plan for this year, which starts this day. I choose to plant good things today and help me to build good foundations to do your perfect will. In Christ name, AMEN

CHAPTER TWENTY SIX
Two Ways: Wide and Easy or Narrow and Difficult

Scripture Foundation

Romans 6:23-For the wages of sin is death, but the gift of God is eternal life in Christ Jesus our Lord.

Matt. 7:13.14-"Enter by the narrow gate; for wide is the gate and broad is the way that leads to destruction, and there are many who go in by it. Because narrow is the gate and difficult is the way which leads to life, and there are few who find it.

SECRET: FREE WILL TO CHOOSE IS GOD'S HEART

Just so happens as I'm writing that a gallon of gas is $2.22. Really, 22 is not my favorite number, and you may or may not be impressed by the 22 thing. My point is: your secret may come through another number, or an animal, or a color, or history, etc.

But I would like to emphatically tell you that you were created in your mom's womb to unveil secrets. But this won't be easy. I was married at 22, as with any, it could have been destroyed in short order, but I've enjoyed 38 plus years with the same wonderful woman. I love you Honey!! I pray that the LIGHT of God's Word would conquer and overwhelm any CONFUSION! I am not afraid of chaos, confusion, disorder, Pride, and unbelief. In Jesus name I look at it, expose It, put His light on it and remove it from every part of my life. I am made in His image, He looked at chaos, and spoke light, and spoke the worlds into being.

A simple truth my friend. Are you a baby Christian? Follow the word. Choose a destiny with His word and light. Are you a spiritual teen? My observation in 40+ years of ministry is that 80% of people in the church are Spiritual teenagers. Stuck in between baby and a Spirit functional, fruitful Christian. I have an insatiable desire to push you to the next level of "SON". It is time to get rid of the bottle and start chewing on meat (solid food) Hebrews 5:14. So a "Huios (Greek)" son is where we are headed. Led by the Spirit (Romans 8:14) Most Christians are still on a skim milk bottle, or stuck. And I mean STUCK!!! We are striving for the identity of a son that will be skilled in spirit, soul, and body. Do you want Him to deal with you as a son giving you responsibility, or a child? A final stage of biblical maturity is "pater" Greek for a mature Christian who molds like a potter, balanced, and according to James 1, and 2 Peter 1, lacking nothing. We will get into those chapters in book number 2.

This is about attitude and the moral compass of how you look at life. If the first time you hit a bump in the road, you cave in, the miracle of faith that is motivated by hope is very weak in your foundation. Mark chapter 11, a seed on the end of your finger, that is the quantity of faith you need to move mountains. But wrong motives are keeping us from faith.

When it comes down to it, there are only two attitudes towards God. We can honor Him, or we can hate Him. Psalm 50:23 says, 'Those who sacrifice thank-offerings honor me' He contrasts those who 'hate my instruction' in (v.17a).

Two types of ground to stand on: holy or hidden. Is there any area of your life that you keep hidden because it is a place of secret sin? In Joshua, we see two contrasting kinds of ground. We see Joshua standing on holy ground (Joshua 5:15). On the other hand, we see Achan standing on the ground of hidden sin (Joshua 7:21–22).

When this mystery is finished, I think you will be quite impressed to what lengths the Father would go to show that He cares about purging my ground. NO, I have never heard of THE FAITH IN PURITY 2:22, but as I was searching, it popped up. It came out of my hunger to uncover secrets. Please join in my secret. MAY OUR PASSION BE ONLY CHRIST. WE WILL HAVE ONE OF TWO CHOICES, OUR GARMENTS SPOTTED, OR OUR GARMENTS PURE WHITE WHEN HE RETURNS!

Jesus himself said that – ultimately – there are only two ways to live: there are two paths; there are two gates; there are two destinations and there are two groups of people. Those on the left. "goats", those on the right, "sheep". They travel on either the broad road, or the narrow road.

Albert Einstein said, 'There are only two ways to live your life. One is as though nothing is a miracle. The other is as though everything is a miracle. Maybe Albert wasn't so amazingly brilliant after all, maybe it was a secret called miracles. Jehovah gives two options through Moses: these words, blessing & curses, "life or death", Choose blessing, choose life.

Then He who sat on the throne said, "Behold, I make all things new." And He said to me, "Write, for these words are true and faithful."

Revelations 21:5-8-And He said to me, "It is done!

THE FAITH IN PURITY

I am the Alpha and the Omega, the Beginning and the End. I will give of the fountain of the water of life freely to him who thirsts. He who overcomes shall inherit all things, and I will be his God and he shall be My son. 8. But the cowardly, unbelieving, abominable, murderers, sexually immoral, sorcerers, idolaters, and all liars shall have their part in the lake which burns with fire and brimstone, which is the second death."

The goal of this book is of course, teaching and spurring you on toward faith in purity. If somehow you are not clear, there are two possible destinations, heaven, and hell. You say, how do I know that something I did will not send me to hell? It's about LAW, and GRACE. If your teen did a terrible wrong, and showed up at your door, it's your choice. Bye, never want to see you again. I DON'T THINK SO. They have not lost their place in your home, they have missed the mark, and things must get right. So it is with the Father, get right with him and enter into His Kingdom, THE FAITH IN PURITY!

Holy Spirit- Let me believe and live your miracle of Grace. I will swim against the flow of chaos; I will choose the straight and narrow. I choose Your discipline to get off skim milk, and listen to your every command today. I am your sheep, and I hear your voice every day. I choose to be faithful. I choose to be your son, led by you Holy Spirit, In Christ name I pray, AMEN

CHAPTER TWENTY SEVEN
Exposing Shame

SCRIPTURE FOUNDATION

TITUS 1:15A--TO THE PURE ALL THINGS ARE PURE, BUT TO THOSE WHO ARE DEFILED--AND UNBELIEVING NOTHING IS PURE

SECRET: PROVERBS 11:1,2 - GOD HATES PEOPLES UNEVEN WEIGHTS, PRIDE IS A PARTNER TO SHAME

Make it clear, the gateway to God's kingdom is repentance. We must define and expel the sin and strongholds in our life. The erosion of morals, and respect, the entrance of the internet, social chit chat has sabotaged God's voice. Interestingly, the first definition of passion in the dictionary is "strong and barely controllable emotion." Barely controllable. So the word lust is very appropriate here, but this word seems to always have a connotation of sexual addiction (which clearly fits), but the question, what is your passion? Blessed are the pure in heart, for they will see God- Matt. 5:6. Oh to follow purity, and to clearly see the Father, and hear him.

I was born again at 9 and then had a renewal experience at 11 and 15. I encourage you to earmark those moments in your life. I remember what happened in my heart on those 3 occasions and it was needed for me to move on. But I was always affected by a horrible experience that I had when I was about 7. I have always said, how can I expect others to be transparent if I am not? A powerful rule for purity: expose shame, don't hide it. In just one incident a young man invaded my private world in our home, and this defiling experience began a stronghold in my flesh. I imagine my siblings reading this are wondering why they had never heard about this. Shame creates hidden secrets in most people's lives. We tend to think that; to expose these things is not faith. It is just not easy for honest exchange in these matters. Faith is asking you to open up these doors!

The truth is, I don't really know what happened. My best description, I received glasses that caused me not to see everything right. This became a secret chamber in me that cried for healing. Shame is a root system with fear and must be destroyed. Secret things happen to most, most don't find resolve at the cross. They push it under, and the

THE FAITH IN PURITY

pain causes a state as mentioned in our text. Titus 1:15, To the pure all things are pure, but to those who are defiled, and unbelieving nothing is pure; but even their mind and conscience are defiled. KEY POINT! The bible does not say that you are evil because you are defiled and unbelieving, it says "nothing is pure with this person." It also does not say that you are evil because your conscience is defiled. But those problems must be resolved. "DEFILEMENT AND UNBELIEF ARE TWINS, AND PARTNERS TO DESTROY YOUR FAITH, NO MATTER IF THE SOURCE IS YOUR FAULT OR SOMEONE ELSE'S." Stop beating yourself up! There is no condemnation in Christ! Condemnation will be the secret agent to keep you defiled, and unbelieving, and impure. Matthew 15:8a-9, 17-18. "These people draw near to Me with their mouth, and honor Me with their lips, but their heart is far from Me. Do you not yet understand that whatever enters the mouth goes into the stomach and is eliminated? But those things which proceed out of the mouth come from the heart, and they defile a man."

You say, but I can't stop feeling condemnation. 2 Corinthians 5:21, then put on righteousness.

I have no business highlighting the source of your defilement, or the reason for your passion. You must do that with a trusted Godly person. I desire to direct you over and over, and over that your passion would be GOD'S WORD.

The revelation He has given me is "The Faith in Purity." So, if I have been hurt, defiled, and have had bad deals, I cannot have strong faith? I am telling you just the opposite of that. My greatest heroes with the strongest passion for Jesus have gone through the gift of woundedness, and through the fire. Everything is a miracle, especially His grace, forgiveness, and deliverance. The Holy Spirit turned what the enemy meant for evil, and made it good.

Holy Spirit, may this study bring a desire to wash the soul clean (Heb 10:22.) "Let us draw near with a true heart in full assurance of faith, having our hearts sprinkled from an evil conscience and our bodies washed with pure water." I visit the place of my shame, and I ask you to remove it. I renounce the pride that would cause me to remain a victim. I am entitled to healing that came from Jesus' wounds, and beatings. I daily apply the Word of God that you give me. Shame doesn't live here no more, when your Name was spoken, your Love brought healing to me.   In Jesus Name AMEN

CHAPTER TWENTY EIGHT
Pulling Down Strongholds

Scripture Foundation

2 Corinthians 10:4a For the weapons of our warfare are not carnal but mighty in God for pulling down strongholds.

SECRET: HEBREWS 12:1,2 PASSED AWAY SAINTS SURROUND US, STRONGHOLDS FALLS FROM US, AND SHACKLES FALL FROM OUR FEET!

A stronghold can be positive, or negative. Several references to strongholds in the Old Testament are positive. Psalm 18:2 "The LORD is my rock and my fortress and my deliverer; My God, my strength, in whom I will trust; My shield and the horn of my salvation, my stronghold."

A stronghold exists in a person's mind; it includes houses of thoughts constructed in the mind. You have one of two choices, will those strongholds be THE WORD, or fleshly playgrounds for the enemy? So do not let a negative one grow into a generational curse. The following has been around the body of Christ for decades, but bears repeating. What you expose yourself to positive, or negative will govern your THINKING, you're thinking will determine your DECISIONS, your decisions will determine your ACTIONS your actions will determine HABITS your habits will determine CHARACTER your character will determine your DESTINY. (your job to find the Scriptures for each of these.)

I have often thought, what happened to that young man that brought him to hurt me? What caused his destiny to destroy others? Someone taught him destructive thoughts, actions, and habits. Look at Heb. 11: the people of GREAT faith have experienced great hardship to achieve it. We must expose hidden wounds and then apply the Word, Word, Word. 2 Corinthians 10:4,5 – For the weapons of our warfare are not carnal but mighty in God for pulling down strongholds, casting down arguments and every high thing that exalts itself against the knowledge of God, bringing every thought into captivity to the obedience of Christ.

Notice that WE MUST DO the PULLING and the CASTING with His weapons. So, the delivering blow to the enemy is the PURE FLOW of God's Word. I have mentioned my journey of battles when I was 18 years old. I was a chaotic basket case. BUT I had a job with a giant saw buzzing all day long. I will reemphasize and mention, I prayed in the Holy Spirit, and I memorized lots of scripture. Oh, the titanic battles as I prayed and quoted scripture. Many strongholds were destroyed in those years. Two ROCKS were planted in my foundation, PRAYER, and the WORD. Don't ever forget the big three, PRAYER, WORD, and out of those 2 will come the right FELLOWSHIP!

As you define THE FAITH IN PURITY, there may be no greater revelation than this. If I am defiled, my conscience will not allow me to have GREAT FAITH. The thing that has taken me a lifetime to understand is; when I was born again and received forgiveness through the blood of Jesus, he forgave me and made me clean, no matter the origin of that sin. The hard truth is; when we are transgressed upon, the first problem is acknowledging MY sin. But you don't know what they did? Listen, we all have sinned, but really, the difference sometimes is simply acknowledging your sin! Jesus hung on the cross with spikes in His forgiving extremities, and we spend a lifetime trying to vindicate our dysfunctional life, and hatred. Entitlement is a subject for another time, but you are entitled to God's blood bought WORD! We must say what Jesus said, "Father forgive them for they know not what they do! SHAME

AND FEAR WEAKEN WHEN WE FORGIVE "His righteousness in you will become evident." He made you righteous when you were born again, this is about you recognizing it. When that man sinned against me, it became my sin, it became my stronghold from the enemy. When I forgave, shame and its shackles weakened, then as I applied His Word over time those chains were broken. HALLELUJAH!

Holy Spirit, I am daily dying to those old thought patterns, and I ask you to help so they don't rise and defeat me today. I cast down imaginations, and pull down strongholds. I acknowledge my sin, I am entitled to your blood bought forgiveness. I WILL STAY VIOLENT, AND OFFENSIVE WITH HIS WORD, HIS BLOOD, AND HIS NAME! I take refuge in You, the Shield and the Horn of my Salvation, my STRONGHOLD! In Christ Name AMEN

CHAPTER TWENTY NINE
Goliath Must Fall, (Part 1)

Scripture Foundation

1 Samuel 17:10,11 And the Philistine said, "I defy the armies of Israel this day; give me a man, so that we may fight together." When Saul and all Israel heard these words of the Philistine, they were dismayed and greatly afraid.

Genesis 50:20 But as for you, you meant evil against me; but God meant it for good, in order to bring it about as it is today, to save many people alive.

SECRET: GOLIATH DEFINITION: TO UNCOVER, TO REVEAL

My friend, please let the Holy Spirit unveil and discover the secret of the hardest moments in your life. The terrible accident, or tragic death of a loved one. Cancer, covid, financial ruin, or abuse, moments of rage, religious hypocrites that made you hate Christianity. I am here to tell you that God is good. Make it clear, he cannot do evil, and cannot tempt you with evil. So, at whatever point of pain or fear or shame you are regarding your "life bombs" I am asking Holy Spirit to unlock and unveil divine secrets out of your tragedy.

I am so thankful for one of the most difficult moments in my life. The Lord did not invite evil to visit me, I was living, and I ran into evil, and it defiled me. It became my hurt, and my responsibility to hide, or expose my pain, choose life, or choose death. The Father directed me to face Goliath to uncover and reveal the incredible DESTINY OF MY LIFE.

I have called him many things, but I will call him Goliath. As I speak of this person, please understand that the spirit of Goliath was my true foe, not a person. I grew up in a beautiful family with strong bible foundations, my lions and bears would be defined as adolescent fear, shame, and insignificance, and probably a god called sports. What were yours called? It is my prayer that this man will read this someday, that he would know that his hurt became the greatest revelation, blessing, and lesson in my life. I would not sue him; I would embrace and affirm him, buy him a cup of coffee.

Junior high school is bad enough for most. I was

a social misfit, kind of a nerd. A 1.5 GPA, D- nerd but I could shoot a basketball, and had inherent athletic ability, and I guess some singing skills. However, even standing in gym class and having my shorts pulled down to the floor by Goliath, well, it hindered everything. Guys, remember the jock strap that every boy needed to wear (don't ask me why) well, everybody saw it. Everybody saw the absolute humiliation as I made a wrong turn into the gym during lunch, and there Goliath stood (with his hoods), and screamed, "Pomp you're a loser!" And oh, I remember his profanity. He would come from the blindside, and with his fist, blast me in my shoulder, and I would fall to the ground in pain. I did not know that the Holy Spirit was right there with me all the time. My confidence failed, and plummeted, and Goliath was giving me advanced skills of anger, fear, and shame that could destroy my life. These are the roots that could have made my wife a victim, my jobs a disaster, and character, defiled. (Hebrews 12:15) I would arrive each day at a place of hopelessness and hidden in my hurting heart was insignificance. All this was hidden by most, and I could function in my home and play backyard everything and hide all the pain. This was not the fault of mom, dad, siblings, society, or church. Evil was lurking in order to destroy my life, BUT GRACE WOULD WIN! Grace for me would come through the faint loving voice of the Holy Spirit. I had no one to talk to and no counselors. Months after this incident Father brought me mentors, bible studies, and love for worship that would set my life course. In context to family and friends, at all costs, figure out a way to communicate with your loved ones spirit-to-spirit. Proverbs 4:24-TPT-Pay attention to the welfare of your innermost being, for out of there flows the wellspring of life. I believe out of this wellspring is THE FAITH IN PURITY. Don't ever underestimate the power and blessing of spirit exchange, friendships, and mentors.

However for me, this Goliath was one that the Father needed me to face alone.

So came the moment. In the bible it was David facing this giant in front of everyone. King David was always alone in the field with his sheep. God showed him kingship, and war, and worship in that secluded place. In my quiet place, I was lonely, and afraid, and not yet free from that lion when I was 7 years old. I did not know how to fight hopelessness. I did however have a dad that preached the gospel, and a mom who NEVER stopped praying. I HAD A WORD OF PURE HOPE!

Holy Spirit, I now renounce fear, because you in me will face Goliath, as we have faced the bear and lion. The enemy's speaking voice, and his intimidation will no longer affect me. Grace wins through the blood of Jesus. As Joseph was near death, pits, and prison, God turned it for the good. I trust the same in my life. May HOPE become faith in me. In Christ Name AMEN.

CHAPTER THIRTY
Goliath Must Fall (Part 2)

Scripture Foundation

Isaiah 53:5,6 Surely He has borne our griefs and carried our sorrows; yet we esteemed Him stricken, smitten by God, and afflicted. But He was wounded for our transgressions, He was bruised for our iniquities, the chastisement for our peace was upon Him, and by His stripes we are healed.

Acts 7:59,60- And they stoned Stephen as he was calling on God and saying, "Lord Jesus, receive my spirit." Then he knelt down and cried out with a loud voice, "Lord, do not charge them with this sin." And when he had said this, he fell asleep.

SECRET: THE SECRET OF THE LORD IS WITH THOSE WHO FEAR HIM, AND HE WILL SHOW THEM HIS COVENANT

Goliath, to uncover, to reveal. Incredible if the destiny of my life was to be a minister of

Hope, and worshiper, and a warrior, well those things may have never been revealed without facing Goliath. My current condition while facing him was fear, shame, and insignificance. Yes, he always kicks you the hardest when you're down.

   I was in a weight room, alone. It would be the final test to break me and destroy the little confidence I had. I was standing against a wall. Goliath came as a coward from behind, and with pointed cowboy boots, kicked me with all his might in my behind parts. With great accuracy I might add. This state wrestling champion couldn't even wait for me to turn around and punch me in the face. The pain, though intense, maybe was not as bad as his address. "Pomp, you're a #$%@ pathetic loser." I was on the floor in shock and awe, and for the first time in my life, anger had grown into murder. He bolted, and as I gingerly walked home with ill intent fully pregnant in me. I remember plopping on the bed in incredible pain. Please stay with me and don't feel sorry for me. But consider the options of one who is in the middle of a horrifying trial. Remember I will never leave you or forsake you! Deuteronomy 31:8. Consider this horrifying moment that the Lord turned out for my good. A life miracle was about to take place. I would stand in the Lord's presence with Goliath's head in my hand, (spiritually) with the revelation that it had nothing to do with this hurting boy in my class. NOTHING!

So, the angel of the Lord and Holy Spirit appeared in my room. No not physically, but later I would recognize this miracle. In rage, I visualized the gun in my dad's closet, and knives in the drawer. How could I find his house and how could I get there? Then it was like Father gently picking me up and setting me in a swivel chair. A prophetic act was about to take place that would change my life. It's like Father God was standing behind this chair, and gently turning it 45 degrees, then 90 degrees. And I screamed "no, (because I suddenly knew what He was doing). I will not forgive him; I must get him back"! The chair kept turning 180 degrees until my perspective had changed from Goliath to a place on the other wall that was clearly "the Cross". My flesh continued to rage, and I could hear the epic words of Christ, "Father forgive them for they know not what they do." I continued to fight this supernatural council session. No, I can't, I can't, I won't!! Finally, I melted and yielded to the Holy Spirit who comforted me and removed the rage at the Cross. I cried, and He met me there, and He embraced me. My fear turned from goliath to Golgotha, THE FEAR OF THE LORD. PSALM 25:14-THE SECRET OF THE LORD IS WITH THOSE WHO FEAR HIM, AND HE WILL SHOW THEM HIS COVENANT

My rage turned into an absolute HOPE that

would mold my destiny. Hope (the make-up of faith) was truly birthed in me that day. My journey now started to turn hope into faith. To know that He was there, and He knew that this bruise would become my healing. I suddenly knew at that moment that my worth was incredible, He paid for it. I also knew that I needed not be afraid of Goliath anymore. Incidentally, he never bothered me again.

Oh, Holy Spirit, let me know that you want to unveil the secrets of my wounds, and tragedies. I turn to the cross, knowing that it will lead to the resurrection. I relinquish my right and entitlement to stay stuck in my tragedy. I call on grace in my situation, and pain. You have placed me in this world, and its pain is teaching me to HIDE MYSELF IN YOU. I FORGIVE AS YOU FORGAVE, AND AS STEPHEN FORGAVE, AND AS JOSEPH YOU TURN OUT ALL THINGS FOR MY GOOD! HALLELUJAH, IN CHRIST NAME, AMEN

CHAPTER THIRTY ONE
THE SIN OF THE RELIGIOUS SPIRIT (PART 1)

SCRIPTURE FOUNDATION

MATTHEW 23:27 FOR YOU ARE LIKE WHITEWASHED TOMBS WHICH INDEED APPEAR BEAUTIFUL OUTWARDLY, BUT INSIDE ARE FULL OF DEAD MEN'S BONES AND ALL UNCLEANNESS.

SECRET: A CHILD, SMALL ON THE OUTSIDE, GOD'S DNA ON THE INSIDE. THE RELIGIOUS SPIRIT, PRETTY ON THE OUTSIDE, UGLY ON THE INSIDE!

When a religious spirit causes you to judge others, and be prideful, let me tell you, that is a stronghold that is very unpleasant to the Father. OH, WAS JESUS MAD at verbal abusers, users, and posers with religious robes on! The seat of compromise, false religion, pride, lukewarmness, and stunted growth are based in a religious spirit. I would conclude that FEAR is at the seat of this pride. FEAR OF MAN, FEAR OF GIVING UP CONTROL! When anger, and rage have caused you to ruin many relationships in your life, the fruit of the Holy Spirit must take over this pattern. STOP JUDGING PEOPLE! (Matt. 7:1) Religious spirits destroy pure faith!

It doesn't matter where this slithering religious snake came from, IT must BE REMOVED by Christ's blood!!!! The culture of this religious thing is pretense, not revealing what is really on the inside. More definitions of pretense: insincere behavior, not genuine, unwarranted claim, a claim with few facts. And let's again define defraud. After much study, here is my detailed definition of defraud. To cheat like Pharaoh, to get deceitfully, a poisonous hurt, and leading someone, or yourself to a place where they cannot righteously fulfill their desires. Cheating others and drawing them into your desires, so that they cannot righteously fulfill their desires. Cheating yourself, by bearing your own light (like lucifer) so that you cannot righteously fulfill your desires. The blood of Jesus must break the confusion, fear, impurity, pride, and SHAME'S stronghold!

TWO TYPES OF SIN

So, what is the difference between "sin" and "sin"?

1. The most serious sin possible is the one

of pride, and rejection of the Creator, Savior, Redeemer. This is a sin that will send you to hell without yielding your heart to Christ. (Rom 6:23a) The wages of sin is death. To close out this thought Rev 21:8- "But the cowardly, unbelieving, abominable, murderers, sexually immoral, sorcerers, idolaters, and all liars shall have their part in the lake which burns with fire and brimstone, which is the second death." So, if the sin of pride has kept you from receiving Christ into your life, (believing that He died and rose from the dead) Please receive Him. But please note the big serious sins are lumped with the cowardly and the liars in that previous verse. Simple innocent lies can be disgusting to the Holy Spirit. One who is CONVERTED, must be translated from the power of darkness to the Kingdom of His Son. Col 1:13 The destination of lives lived with intentional blatant sins is "hell". Salvation will change the CULTURE from death to life, choose life.

2nd, the sin after one becomes a child of God. This book is about "purity," dealing with this sin, dividing light and darkness in your life, and embracing the light. This is a story of myself receiving a miracle download to help me apply ointment to negative strongholds in my life, the ointment is God's Word. I hate the religious spirit- 1. The religious spirit takes away from the life and power of the church and feeds the pride James 1:27. 2. If our spiritual posture is pride, it may be our downfall. Isaiah 14:12-20 3. The religious spirit assumes that you already know God's opinion 1 Corinthians 5:6 4. The religious spirit is usually found in zeal for God. Zeal is not always good. Matthew 23;12 5. When the religious spirit succeeds, it brings about perfectionism, "I am better than you". Luke 9:48

So as Jesus gazed at the Pharisees and Sadducees, oh He didn't like the fruit that he saw. I love John the Baptist's conclusion of the Kingdom. Matthew 3:8a says, Therefore bear fruits worthy of repentance. Let's look at the fruits of the Holy Spirit in Galatians chapter 5. Below in the first column are the Spirit fruits, in the 2nd column are the enemies of those fruits. In the 3rd column we have the result of pressing through the enemy's camp and arriving in God's kingdom. Your job, find scriptures for each of these things.

LOVE, FEAR, COMPASSION

JOY, DEPRESSION, STRENGTH, SUSTENANCE

PEACE, STORMS,UNREST, RIGHTEOUSNESS

PATIENCE, ANGER, WISDOM

KINDNESS, PRETENSE, GOD'S MOTIVES

GOODNESS, VENGEANCE, REPENTANCE

MEEKNESS, UNYIELDING, ANOINTING

FAITHFULNESS, DOUBT, OBEDIENCE
SELF CONTROL, LUST-DEFRAUD, PURITY

Holy Spirit, reveal to me places in my life where I am posing, and not genuine. Lord, let me never lead myself, or others to a place where righteousness cannot prevail. I renounce the religious spirit, and pride that would destroy, THE FAITH IN PURITY. I choose to be the greatest servant of all. In Christ name AMEN!

CHAPTER THIRTY TWO
The Sin Of The Religious Spirit (Part 2)

Scripture Foundation

Matthew 7:1 Judge not lest you be judged.

SECRET: DANIEL 2:22-HE REVEALS PROFOUND AND HIDDEN THINGS, HE KNOWS WHAT IS IN THE DARK.

SECRET: ISAIAH 45:3-HE GIVES YOU TREASURES OF DARKNESS AND HIDDEN WEALTH IN SECRET PLACES, HE CALLS YOU BY NAME.

I want to again address the religious lie that tries to point the finger at a certain sin. We just addressed the two kinds of sin. 1. The sin of rejecting Christ, result; hell! 2. The everyday sin after one has received Christ, (RESULT) 1Jn 1:9 if you confess your sin, He will always forgive, He gives you a new (culture) robe of righteousness, and that is how He sees you. (my paraphrase) Most

THE FAITH IN PURITY

believe that there is something extra bad about sexual sins, or drugs, alcohol, and today's gay and lesbian. Jesus was ruthless to the Pharisees"! He would display total grace to a stealing tax collector, or a swindler named Zaccheaus in a tree, or a prostitute thrown out in a street. But Matthew 23- "Woe to you, scribes and Pharisees, hypocrites! For you travel land and sea to win one proselyte, and when he is won, you make him twice as much a son of hell as yourselves. "Woe to you, scribes and Pharisees, hypocrites! And that's only a fraction of that chapter.

We cannot overlook this picture of Jesus' fury. When was He really ticked? At religious big mouths who were throwing the adulterer in the street, they were snakes, and dead on the inside. He didn't scream, He knelt down on the ground and wrote they're girlfriend's name in the sand. Or maybe it was the name of the guy who was with the adulterer that they threw in the street. They had their big fingers stuck so securely in everyone's face, and they couldn't see they were on their way to hell and dragging folks with them. Shout it loud, the Spirit of Christ does not tolerate this form of impurity. True religion is visiting widows and orphans, and keeping yourself unspotted from the world. James 1:27. This person will walk up to Jesus with a smile at the judgment seat, and He will say, I never knew you.

THE FAITH IN PURITY

The following story is the most powerful story in my life of the Holy Spirit addressing the religious spirit. So this journey is about secrets. The question; when He begins to unfold a secret, are you willing to watch the secret unveil, even though you don't like it so much?

I was part of an incredible camp in which I ministered to 150-300 teens for twelve years in a row. Many were saved, healed, and delivered. I was so privileged to be a part of this movement! One such year I would be co-speaker with a man who had not been too many years out of prison. He had a world-wide ministry in like five years, and the Lord was about to show me a lesson about my inward condition. I have never been prejudiced or had any major judgment about people. I was in youth ministry for 25 years. I began my week, considering this guy a murderer, with a miracle exit from prison. It seemed to me that this guy wasn't ready to do what he was doing. And that was pretty much before I met him. I would smile and act like I was enjoying myself, but inside was something wrong. So, the next morning I sat there in the 3rd row, and Father showed me a vision. As I was sitting there, I saw the 3 crosses, and what was about to unfold would change my life. Jesus of course was in the middle, and of course on one side was this man that I was looking at and listening to. I kind of nodded my head, and said, yup, there he is, a sinner, tattoos and all, and I do feel sorry for him. Then to my utter horror I glanced over, and there on the other cross was me. Even worse than that, I was wearing a 3-piece suit: (Really!) Oh, I occasionally like to wear a suit. Immediately the drama unfolded, and I looked to Jesus and pleaded, get us down right now, it's me, your son Timothy. I saw myself as a very unhappy camper in a tie and going crazy over my predicament. In my insolence, I forgot that He was saving the world. Hello McFly, this is one of the most important moments in history. Reading the scripture, this pleading man on the wrong side of Jesus was committing blasphemy. Then tears began to fall in that service as I put my hands in my face, I realized my disgusting motives. Other things happened, and "then in real time" out of the other sinner's mouth came the unadulterated beautiful prayer, "REMEMBER ME". And Jesus' response, "today you will be with me in paradise." Clearly, He did not say that to me. I suddenly realized that my posing, and hypocrisy were deadly to me. He was a forgiven murderer, I was a judge, with absolute wrong motives and pride. My sin was putrid to Him. Jesus forgave me too. And I would grow to love and respect this man in the upcoming days. Today He's riding his Harley in paradise on streets of gold.

We need to know the meaning of words, and we need to know how those definitions play out in your character. Let's again reflect on the 5 phases of pride, and they're bible counterparts.

1 Pride------------------- Humility-1 Peter 5:5,6

2 Independence---------- Meekness-1Peter 3:4

3 Selfishness----------- Brokenness-Psalms 51:17

4 Conceit---------------- Contrite-Psalms 34:18

5 Pretense---------------- Purity-Philippians 4:8

Holy Spirit, I judge myself, and I will carefully guard my thoughts toward others. I break the power of the ugly drama, posing, pretentious spirit that will try to break my UNION with you. When you unveil things to me, I will cast down pride, and be willing to submit to your Word. I take off the mask, and to you I expose every room in my heart that is unclean. In Christ Name, AMEN

CHAPTER THIRTY THREE
Partners With Conscience

Scripture Foundation

James 1:15 "Then, when lust (wrong passion) has conceived, it gives birth to sin; and sin, when it is full-grown, brings forth death." The reciprocal: When Christ's (passion) is conceived, it brings forth righteousness. His grown-up Kingdom is righteousness, peace, and Joy in the Holy Spirit.

Hebrews 9:14 no more conscience of sin-

SECRET: 1 CORINTHIANS 2:10 (TPT) BUT GOD NOW UNVEILS THESE PROFOUND REALITIES TO US BY THE SPIRIT. YES HE HAS REVEALED TO US HIS INMOST HEART AND DEEPEST MYSTERIES. THROUGH THE HOLY SPIRIT WHO EXPLORES ALL THINGS.

What is YOUR conscience? The conscience is the voice that monitor's the purity of your PASSION. The Holy Spirit will tell you that conscience can be the greatest tool in your life to THE FAITH IN PURITY. A good conscience can be the thermostat, to gauge the temperature of your temple! If you are dealing with religious bigotry, tobacco, anger, or lust, murder, cowardice, or white lies, here is the pattern.

When a stronghold brings your desires and thoughts above or against God's Word, that is LUST. We used to call lust "an act of your thoughts past temptation." My friend, do not be afraid of it, do not make excuses, just expose it; do not let it continue. Then, LUST brings you to a point of action, which is SIN. And when sin (separation from Father) is finished, it brings death. But it was not my fault! It does not matter, Chances are it was grandpa, or grandma's stronghold passed on to you. It will never matter! IT MUST BE DEALT WITH.

Jesus totally removes the guilt and shame, symptoms arise, but they flee at the entrance of His word, (Psalm 119:130)

Conscience plus Holiness- 1 Pet 1:13-16-Therefore gird up the loins of your mind, be sober, and rest your hope fully upon the grace that is to be brought to you at the revelation of Jesus Christ; as obedient children, not conforming yourselves to the former lusts, as in your ignorance; but as He who called you is holy, you also be holy in all your conduct, because it is written, "Be holy, for I am holy." Any vice that works against the Light of Jesus in you can be this lust.

A thought from Oswald Chambers. God's highest glory is His Holiness. Holy hates and destroys the evil and works the good. In man, conscience has the same work: it condemns sin and approves the right. Rom. 9:1. I say the truth in Christ, I lie not, my conscience also bearing me witness in the Holy Ghost-

Conscience plus the HOLY SPIRIT- 'The Spirit Himself bears witness with our spirit.'-Rom 8:16. Conscience is the remains of God's image in man, the nearest approach to the Divine in him. Therefore, God's work of redemption must always begin with conscience. (Chambers) For you were bought at a price; therefore, glorify God in your body and in your spirit, which are God's. 1 Corinthians 6:19

Conscience plus the BLOOD OF JESUS--'A heart sprinkled from an evil conscience,' 'having no more conscience of sin' (Heb. 9:14, 10: 2, 22), Conscience is meant to be the privilege of every believer. When conscience joins with the Power of Jesus' Blood. The reality of redemption is that we can experience it, hallelujah! (Chambers)

Six powerful benefits of the blood- 1. The blood of Jesus affirms your redemption. Ephesians

1:7. 2. - He purchased the whole church with his blood. Acts 20:28 3. His blood breaks down walls. Ephesians 2:13,14. 4. His blood cleanses us from sin. 1 John 1:9. 5. His blood overcomes Satan. Rev.12:11. 6. His blood gives us access to the Holy of holies. Heb 10:19

CONSCIENCE PLUS LOVE. -1 Tim 1:5, Now the purpose of the commandment is love from a pure heart, from a good conscience, and from sincere faith,19-having faith, and a good conscience, which some having rejected, concerning the faith have suffered shipwreck, of whom are Hymenaeus and Alexander, whom I delivered to Satan that they may learn not to blaspheme. The Faith in purity is all over these versus. Love forgives no matter what someone has done to you. (1 John 3: 21,22) Holding the mystery of -the faith in a pure conscience. 'Beloved! If our heart condemns us not, we have boldness toward God, because we keep His commandments…When we reach the pinnacle of love, our conscience will be the governor. Everyone will have a test of people who have rejected the faith. But we must be patient, kind, and not notice others' mistakes. Help us Lord.

CONSCIENCE PLUS HUMILITY-How shall we get free from the works of the flesh? Philippians 2:5-9 Let nothing be done through selfish ambition or conceit, but in lowliness of mind let each esteem others better than himself. Let each of you look out not only for his own interests, but also for the interests of others. Let this mind be in you which was also in Christ Jesus, who, being in the form of God, did not consider it robbery to be equal with God, but made Himself of no reputation, taking the form of a bondservant, and coming in the likeness of men. And being found in appearance as a man, He humbled Himself and became obedient to the point of death, even the death of the cross.

Humility is the posture of a pure conscience.

CONSCIENCE PLUS SANCTIFICATION-- For this is the will of God, your sanctification: that you should abstain from sexual immorality; that each of you should know how to possess his own vessel in sanctification and honor, 1 Thessalonians 4:3- (Rom. 8: 13 For if you live according to the flesh you will die; but if by the Spirit you put to death the deeds of the body, you will live.----He has called me to be set apart, sanctified. In His work of renewal, the Holy Spirit does not take you in a room and replace you into a new man. He works through man's will. He renews and sanctifies what you bring to Him. Conscience is the voice in you, of the Spirit of God the Creator. What is the difference between your conscience and that of a heathen? Your conscience joins with holiness, Holy Spirit, the blood of Jesus, love, humility, and sanctification. The first care of the Spirit of God is to restore what sin has defiled. Something that we fail to mention enough is destiny. All this process is working to send you into the fullness of your gifts. The stature of the fullness of Christ.

Conscience plus confession-With every sin I commit, the light that shines in makes it manifest and condemns it. If the sin is not confessed and forsaken, the stain remains, and conscience becomes defiled, because the mind refused the teaching of the light (Tit. 1:15) To the pure all things are pure, but to those who are defiled and unbelieving nothing is pure; but even their mind and conscience are defiled.

Heb 10:35,36-Therefore do not cast away your confidence, which has great reward. For you have a need of endurance, so that after you have done the will of God, you may receive the promise.

Father, I present to you my inner voice. I humble myself before you, I set myself apart for your glory. I will speak good words that line up with THE FAITH IN PURITY. In Christ name, AMEN!

THE FAITH IN PURITY

CONCLUSION

It is my prayer that as we move on to another subject, THE FAITH IN PURITY, PUTTING CHRIST FIRST, that you will hang with me, and pass on the revelations found. I do know if you pick this up again, you will learn something new again. May His Word change us continually.

I do realize that it is in my DNA to make things deep, and there may be a need to read this one again. I have to blame my mom on something. I have never been accused of being shallow. That is why I made each chapter readable in 5-7 minutes. It is truly my desire to push you to the next level in Christ.

A word that comes to me when reflecting on this book, is the word STUCK. When we look closely at shame and fear, they are powerful agents to hold us up from our potential, goals, and creativity. They weaken our power to OBEY, a very key element of THE FAITH IN PURITY. When I am stuck, I am not creative, patient, or full of Joy. Psalm. 16:11-In His presence is fullness of Joy and at your right hand are pleasures forevermore. You want some secret nuggets, read Psalm 16 in the passion or amplified.

We have in recent chapters reflected on THE RELIGIOUS SPIRIT. I truly believe that this sin is greater than any of the others, not because it is more unforgivable, but because pride is even an older and more putrid sin than SHAME AND FEAR. It was the heart of Lucifer, it was the money behind the rich young ruler, the insolence of Pharaoh, the lukewarm of Revelations 3., And yes the bigotry of the Religious leaders. If you struggle with judgment and a religious spirit as I have, open again, the three doors. REPENTANCE, SALVATION, HUMILITY.

My wife, Cathy, wouldn't want accolades, but through these pages you can probably sense a JOURNEY like no other. Failures, successes, mountains, valleys, mysteries, secrets, and joy unspeakable. Thank you my dear honey we are in this TOGETHER UNTIL THE END. I can't imagine this journey without you. I can't leave out my daddy, who went through WW2 and then headed into a lifetime of ministry. What a foundation OF LOVE. I still wake up some mornings hearing his big booming voice shouting Isaiah 60:1 down the stairs. ARISE AND SHINE FOR THY LIGHT HAS COME, AND THE GLORY OF THE LORD IS RISEN UPON YOU…HA HA HA GOOD MORNING TIM!! And fourteen months ago my mom joined him in eternity, walking the streets of gold. Most secrets and nuggets are mined out in the early morning, right mom?

Finally, I can't help but conclude with GRACE. Grace defines hope. Because of that, Grace defines and must be the posture of your faith. FOR BY GRACE are you saved through FAITH. Moving on to PURITY. It will only be by GRACE that we will stand before the Father with white robes, and He will say, "Well done, good and faithful servant. No, I didn't wash my robes with lye soap. It's all because of the WONDERFUL GRACE OF JESUS, Greater than all my sin. HALLELUJAH, IT REACHES ME. MAY YOU BE BLESSED ON YOUR JOURNEY IN…

THE FAITH IN PURITY

IN HIS BLESSED HOPE,

TIMOTHY POMP